I Told You So!

The sequined sequel to
Don't Ask, Do Tell!

William Bonzo

Don't Ask, Do Tell: When I finally told the military kiss my gay… was published as non-fiction memoir and was so incredulous that most didn't believe a word of it! Even so, they also found it mesmerizing.

Therefore, consider this as a work of fiction. Names, characters, businesses, places, events and incidents are to be assumed as the product of the author's over imagination.

However, any resemblance to actual persons, living or dead, or actual events is no coincidence, and he is privileged to have lived in New Zealand during these events, and honored to have known everyone mentioned in the book.

The information in this book is meant to supplement, not replace, proper "coming out" training. Like any sport involving speed, equipment, balance and environmental factors, "coming out" poses some inherent risk. The author and publisher advise readers to take full responsibility for their safety and know their limits. Before practicing the skills described in this book, be sure that your *equipment* is well maintained.

ISBN: 0983389209

ISBN-13: 9780983389200

Library of Congress Control Number: 2012941583

Menehune Books, Honolulu, HI

FOREWORD

'Knowledge is an enemy to bigotry.'

William Bonzo has, as promised, followed his very popular book *Don't Ask, Do Tell* – that brave little tome that came into print in October 2010 when the debate about gays in the military was raging, a book of honest appraisal of the situation from the probing and entertaining eyes of a man who had successfully served in the military and dared to give the insider picture. Bonzo stated 'I wrote *Don't Ask, Do Tell* after I was outed as a gay man and discharged from the Navy. Had I served my country honorably and patriotically? Absolutely. Is our military in need of talented and well-trained men and women to lead the troops during wartime? Without question. And yet this policy of Don't Ask, Don't Tell systematically forced men and women to either lie about their identities...or be forced out of the service.'

Now he returns with a new book, described as a 'sequined sequel to *Don't Ask, Do Tell*' that opens even more windows not only to the situation of prejudice present in the military but also to the true facts of what happens while serving as an 'openly gay' man in his final tour of duty in the US Navy. It bubbles with Bonzo's inimitable style of prose and shares a road map of how he adjusted to 'coming out' and the manner in which he found happiness at last – living a life of honesty and joy.

Bonzo opens his story in Hawaii with a tender reflection at the graveside of his deceased partner and shares that train of memory with us the reader, taking us back to his aborted attempt to resign from the Navy when he landed in New Zealand to discover his tour of duty was extended for two years while the Operation Deep Freeze in Antarctica usurped all available Navy forces: Bonzo would be in charge of the Commissary! He adjusts to the language and culture and climate of New Zealand in a series of hilarious introductions, finds his assigned staff devoted and friendly, and discovers the beauty of the quality of life in his new home. And then, after his discharge, he elects to stay as long as allowed in his beloved New Zealand.

The remainder of the book details his gradual emergence into the gay life in Christchurch, finding a lover, taking on two teenagers as sons – lads without parents who hung out in the local gay bar, his settling in a new apartment in the common part of town and his transition from a life as a closeted gay man to a popular, warmly loving, exceptionally bright and hunky gay man. The friends he makes and the manner in which he conducts his life weds him to the Isle of New Zealand, a place he would always refer to as home despite the fact that his visas totaled only three years in length. He bids a touching farewell to New Zealand, his partner and his sons, travels to Australia and other ports where he comes to understand the freedom of being a man no longer needing to hide in the closet. This journey is in many ways a story of how one man 'came out' into a world he could barely imagine. And this journey is a rollercoaster ride that eventually returns us to his home in Hawaii – back to the graveside where he starts his memoir, sadly reflecting on the loss of his New Zealand family in the earthquake of February 2011.

One of the many aspects of William Bonzo's writing style is his sprinkling of quotations from a diverse group of people. For instance, while serving in the Navy as an escort to an Admiral he inserts the following quote from Dr. Seuss: 'Be who you are and say what you feel, because those who mind don't matter and those who matter don't mind.' It is that sort of intelligent humor that provides the glowing sequins of this sequel.

William Bonzo has been through the trials of a closeted man in the military and survived, and not only did he survive but he grew in dignity and became an inspiration to all men and women who have found themselves in that prison. But more importantly he has opened that closet door to acceptance and understanding and discovery, sharing the joy of being who he is and finding a world of affection and rewards beyond his expectations. This book is a lighthouse, a tribute, and a nudge in the side as well as a hearty embrace to all his fellow travelers. And as far as this book is concerned, this is one of the most sensitive, hilarious, and warmly pleasurable rides to be released in a long time.

Grady Harp

Grady Harp is a champion of Representational Art in the roles of curator, lecturer, and panelist. He is a writer of art essays, poetry, and critical reviews of literature, art and music. He has produced exhibitions and contributed catalogue essays for the Arnot Art Museum in New York, Fresno Museum of Art, Laguna College of Art and Design, Nevada Museum of Art, National Vietnam Veterans Art Museum in Chicago, and Cleveland State University Art Gallery. He has served as a contributing artistic advisor for universities and colleges throughout California, in Berlin, the Centro Cultural de Conde Duque in Madrid, and for *WAR SONGS; Metaphors in Clay and Poetry from the Vietnam Experience* which toured the United States from 1996-1998. He has provided essays, chapters and introductions to numerous books such as the recent *Powerfully Beautiful* and *100 Artists of the Male Figure* and *Coco: The Testimony of Black and White* – the art of Lita Cabellut published in Paris. He is the art reviewer for Poets & Artists magazine and is the art historian for The Art of Man Quarterly Journal.

"No one can make you feel inferior, without your consent."

Eleanor Roosevelt

DISCLAIMER

There is absolutely none this time.

The military policy of Don't Ask, Don't Tell is history. I have nothing to hide anymore, nor anything to be ashamed of.

I look up from my computer, and out the window of my condo at the Vdara. From Las Vegas, the ninth Hawaiian island, I will unashamedly reveal all.

My gaze flies over the Spring Mountains of Nevada and goes all the way across our country to Washington, DC. Governments may teach their citizens to hate people they have never met, but knowledge is an enemy to bigotry.

There, in the Pentagon, that oddly shaped building with four walls, plus a spare – typical of military thinking and spending, I sincerely hope the Joint Chiefs of Staff, during an analysis of the effect of having allowed Gay and Lesbian patriots to serve openly, will throw my book down on the conference table in the Situation Room and shout at each other until blue in the face "I told you so!"

"Are there any questions about Don't Ask, Do Tell before we move forward to the sequel?"

Q: "In Don't Ask, Do Tell why do you use famous quotes in the beginning of the book, and callout text boxes at the beginning of each chapter?"

A: "Noel Coward once said that 'having to read a footnote resembles having to go downstairs to answer the door while in the midst of making love.' Just consider my lack of foot notes and use of quotes and premature text teasers instead, as foreplay!"

Q: "How did you FINALLY get to warm weather?"

A: "UAL Flight 75, and please don't shout."

Q: "Do you also speak Polish?"

A: "Let me have someone show you the exit."

Q: "Which President are you related to?"

A: "The only one elected to two, nonconsecutive Terms in office."

Q: "So, you like guys with short, military haircuts?"

A: "You try getting thrown into a small room, as I did in Guantanamo Bay, Cuba, fill it with nerve gas and you too will appreciate NOT having long hair, and being able to get a tight seal on the protective mask on your head that stands between you and a horrible, painful death!"

Q: "Will the sequel be full of sequins?"

A: "Do you sew?"

Q: "In New Zealand, do you peek out of the closet, or blow the door off its hinges?"

A: "Do you know any good carpenters?"

Q: "How many do you shag in New Zealand?"

A: "I can't count that high, and I wasn't a swan."

Q: "Will there be a book about your life in Hawaii?"

A: "Hawaii, no ka oi!"

Q: "What do you mean you weren't a swan?"

A: "Swans are monogamous, dear."

Q: "I met you in Vegas recently when you were writing the sequel, and saw you throw a dime you found on the ground into the fountain at the Belagio; what did you wish for?"

A: "This, you, your questions – well, most of them." "That's right, and make sure he doesn't get back in here! Polish…"

Look folks, I know you are all excited about the sequel, but this question and answer session was meant to clarify *Don't Ask, Do Tell.*

My original intent was neither some social commentary, nor a political platform for some jerk in Washington. It was to tell a real story about a slice of military history, from a somewhat different, "colorful" point of view. One does want, after all, a "hint of color," non?

The sequel to *Don't Ask, Do Tell* titled *I Told You So* continues that story, and in celebration of the repeal of the military policy of Don't Ask, Don't Tell now does so WITHOUT the camouflage.

It's twice as long, and twice the fun, so buckle up and enjoy the ride!

Cheers!

"It's not the power of those who oppose you; it's the power you give to those who oppose you."

William Bonzo

CONTENTS

DEDICATION

To all gay men and lesbian women who continue to serve "openly" in our armed forces I say "I'm damned proud of you."

Don't consider our life in the military as a struggle, but as a relentless pursuit of fairness and equality.

It won't be easy to be "out" as there are still many who would rather we were still "in" the closet, or worse. **North Carolina** comes to mind...

I give you credit for you continued courage, and a field manual for your M16 rifle I've amended to read "When carrying your M16, and upon hearing any gay or lesbian slurs, engage the Rai Interface System, then pinpoint the Aimpoint red-dot sight between the eyes of the individual who uttered the slur and respond firmly "You called me what?"

And with tearful eyes, this is dedicated to all who died, and those who remain to carry on, from the tragic events of February, 2011 in my beloved Christchurch, New Zealand where much of the story I am about to tell you takes place.

Following the earthquake, one Kiwi family's humor was endearing:

Maree Butcher said she finds herself shaking awake with memories of February's horror every night. She lies in bed and stares at her husband, Norm, who was nearly killed racing out the back door of their home as the brick walls blew out around him and the top floor collapsed to the ground.

Norm tried to cheer her up, nodding toward the wreckage and saying, "I really did want an *open* entertainment area."

Maree smiled. "We've lost our house and belongings," she sighed, "but we're still alive."

To both Norm and Maree, and all my readers I say "We all eventually die, but not everyone really *lives!*"

And I did live life to its fullest, once upon a time in a land far away called Christchurch, New Zealand...

"My lesbianism is an act of Christian charity. All those women out there praying for a man, and I'm giving them my share."

Rita Mae Brown

Prologue

It's zero dark- thirty; the H-1 highway is deserted. All I see is the front wheel of my Harley as I race alone through the lifeless, black cement canyon of downtown Honolulu. My blank stare reveals nothing of the anguish behind my eyes.

Days before, I had received not from the military, but from his mother who lives in **Laie** on the North Shore, the call I had dreaded. Even though his family is Mormon, and never condoned our lifestyle, Sam and I were undeniably a couple and his mother, at least, acknowledged us as such. The military never would.

The sun is coming up behind me as the exit for Fort Shafter, and the Tripler Army Medical Center looms ahead. How many times had I taken that exit during his hospitalization? I can't count.

Today, though, I would be taking the exit towards Punchbowl Crater.

His **Makuahine's** call is still ringing in my ears.

Now my stare is clouded by tears welling up to the point I can't even see in front of myself. I hadn't been invited to the official burial, yet today, somehow, among all the other servicemen and women who now lie in the National Memorial Cemetery of the Pacific, I find his grave. I miss him.

"Hey Sam," I speak softly to the grave marker now that we can be alone together again, "remember how I used to instruct you that I want to be cremated, and have my ashes spread at Queen's beach, so I would always have a cute guy laying on me?"

The world has stopped as I joke with him. The debate over gay lifestyles with the military and his family is meaningless. I drop to my knees, and stare endlessly towards him. My life sustaining humor fading, I chide him silently that I am the older one, I was supposed to go first, damit!

"You know, Sam" I speak to him now in our usual, casual manner used often together at Bellows Air Force beach, "Life is not about the number of breaths you take, but the moments that take your breath away."

"Fine for you, brah" I imagine him responding in his usual **Hawaiian Pidgin,** "You above da ground!"

I smile in response, and continue our dialogue "For me, besides Hawaii, of course, the most breath taking place on the planet is New Zealand."

I lie back on my elbows, on the perfectly manicured grounds of this military cemetery. I had been prepared to spend a lifetime with him, but now am left to cherish the few years we had together, for a lifetime.

The sun has woken up and is stretching its arms above Diamond Head. The trade winds too seem ready for another days work, air conditioning the island.

I've taken the day off to visit Sam. I strip down to the uniform of the islands; board shorts, tank top and flip-flops. Having removed even those last two garments, which are optional in Hawaii, my toes are wriggling and curling in the grass above him as if they were still intertwined with his in the sand of Bellow's Air Force base beach.

"Since you decided just to lie around here," I chide him, "I have been spending more time at the gym."

"Yea," I continue trying to provoke a response, "I am on a mere 2000 calorie a day diet – I look at the **Zippy's restaurant** ad in da Mid-Week flyer with lust as if I'm looking at porn!"

In his silence I pretend I've made him jealous, and I smile.

I continue speaking playfully to him and say "You know, brah, you weren't the first…"

Making a pillow out of my back-pack, I lay on my back next to Sam. Turning my head towards his marker, I imagine that the trade winds which are gently blowing through the trees above us are his breathing. The warmth of the sun is the warmth of his skin.

Placing my left arm behind my neck for support, I turn my gaze towards the clear blue sky. My right arm falls casually on the grass towards Sam inviting his fingers into mine.

In the comfort of home here in Hawaii, I begin my story of coming out of the military, and the closet simultaneously. The tale will be home to some unique redeeming factors, but it also will pander to my listener by diluting its lesson, which teaches that some comfort zones can only be truly abandoned on a far part of the world.

"The Bible contains six admonishments to homosexuals and 362 admonishments to heterosexuals. That doesn't mean that God doesn't love heterosexuals. It's just that they need more supervision."

William Bonzo

I Told You So

"You are unlikely to have a startling adventure if you never take a more hazardous journey than a train ride from your home to the office."

W. Somerset Maugham

Introduction

Before I met Sam in Hawaii, I had been assigned to Operation Deep Freeze, a "research" mission to Antarctica that was based out of Christchurch, New Zealand.

"Here we go again," I thought. "What, are we planning to invade an iceberg now?" Pre-invasions seemed de-rigueur to me by this point in my military career.

En-route to New Zealand I had resolved, during the long, solitary hours of the flight from Rhein-Main Air Base in Germany, that I would end my long years of running from the military and hiding that I was gay.

Upon arrival in Christchurch I resigned my active duty commission.

My knees weren't shaking.

I quit and it was over, just like that.

Well, not "quite."

I was humbled at their hospitality.

Chapter One: Kia Ora

Our plane touched down on New Zealand's north island at Rongotai International airport in the country's capital Wellington. Actually, it was more like dropping a grand piano from a crane out of a second story window!

As I pulled my face out of the seatback in front of me with my left hand, my right hand motioned ignominiously towards the cockpit. I muttered to the other survivor in the seat next to me "Our pilot must think we are landing on an aircraft carrier."

At a mere 1,936 meters (6,352 feet), Wellington's runway is shorter than even some of New Zealand's domestic airport runways! I felt a sense of deja-vu, and checked my shoes for cow dung.

Still, I gave our pilot approving nods for his skillfulness, simultaneously checking myself for neck injury. The city of Wellington is notorious for high winds which make landing a plane very difficult, reminiscent of the day I had crashed landed a hang glider in a cow pasture in Tennessee.

With Wellington Harbor and Cook Strait to the north and south of the airport respectively, the urgency of getting on the ground is compounded unless you are wearing board shorts and there is a surfboard under your seat in lieu of a regulation flotation device.

An indication of the weather the day we landed came from the smell; winds from the north originating in Rotorua greeted us at Rongotai. While the hot springs there are noted for their therapeutic value, the sulfur aroma can be overwhelming. So if first you die from the smell, you subsequently have healing waters to look forward to!

And one last oddity to this ungracious arrival was that Wellington airport can't be used after 10:30pm. "Next time, just give me a parachute and do a fly-by drop," I suggested to no one in particular as I was suddenly all alone, again, in a foreign country.

"Why is the military always trying to get rid of me?" I puzzled at 10:15 PM in the middle of a Band-Aid sized airstrip. "At least English is spoken here," I comforted myself.

"Kia ora" a man's voice resounded from behind me, and I spun around to see before me a half-naked, dark skinned man with more tattoos on his singular form than on a group of bikers in Hog Heaven (and I don't mean the bar-b-que).

The **Māori's** tattoo their face as a sign of identity. Their term for tattoo is Ta Moko, and each **Moko** tells a unique story. It also shows their rank, their status and their ferocity.

Ancestry is indicated on each side of the face. The left side is generally (but not always, depending on the tribe) the father's side, while the right hand side indicates the mother's ancestry. If one side of a person's ancestry is not of rank, that side of the face has no Moko design.

"I come in peace!" I mustered the courage to stutter four words, and raised the palm of my hand into the air, hoping the gesture wouldn't start a war.

He stuck his tongue out at me.

The Māori people are the indigenous people of **Aotearoa** (New Zealand) and first arrived here in **waka hourua** (voyaging canoes) from their ancestral homeland of **Hawaiki** over 1000 years ago.

I was immediately given the honor to spend a few days at a Māori **marae**, or meeting place. I tried to comfort myself as I was led off the tarmac towards an uncertain fate.

A **powhiri** (formal welcome) at the marae began the following day with a **wero** (challenge). A warrior from the **tangata whenua** (hosts) challenged me, the **manuhiri** (guest). He approached me carrying a **taiaha** (spear) and a token (a small branch) which he laid down in front of me.

I, the manuhiri, was to pick it up to show I in fact came in peace. Of course, in the spirit of international relations and cultural exchange, I reached for the branch, and stuck my tongue out.

Oh no, no, NO! Anyone who watches soccer, and has seen the **Haka**, Maori pre-game war dance, is shaking their head side to side trying to warn me that I made a mistake of international consequence.

Peaceful intentions and friendship having been established none the less, my tongue back in my mouth where it belonged, we embraced. I was humbled at their hospitality. It was, after all, another white man like me who had in 1840, at **The Treaty of Waitangi**, convinced the Māori to cede the sovereignty of New Zealand to Britain.

Having passed my entrance exam to New Zealand I was to fly to Christchurch, located on New Zealand's south island, where Operation Deep Freeze, the National Science Foundation's *research* mission to Antarctica was based. There the airstrip was of adequate length to accommodate our military C-130 cargo planes.

At Rongotai, before I could even utter kia ora to the gate agent, while keeping my tongue in my mouth, I heard someone saying the opposite, **haere ra** and I was shoved hastily into a plane heading south.

"Hey!" I pleaded, "I really do come in peace and the whole tongue thing was just a misunderstanding of local culture on my part."

"Wouldn't a space ship be better suited?" I shouted over the roar of the propeller engines from the back of my head towards the hand that was pushing me head first into the aircraft, "since we are *already* at the World's end!"

I was in love for the
first time.

I Told You So

Chapter Two: The Eagle has Landed

I was dropped in the middle of the remote south island, somewhere between Christchurch and the small town of Dunedin.

"Hey," I shouted towards the plane disappearing over the summit of Mount Cook in the distance, "I was just kidding in Wellington about being dropped from a plane!"

"What's more," I continued fruitlessly shouting at the face of the mountain, the plane having vanished, "check your compass; this isn't Christchurch!"

In mythology the eagle represents might and courage. Although at this moment, I felt neither trait historically associated with this symbol of my home country.

"Hello, little fellow," I continued without missing a beat, now looking down at my feet. "What's your name then, my little feathered friend?" I continued in a softer tone.

I had landed in the domain of the **Kiwi** bird – found only in New Zealand.

The Kiwi bird is semi-nocturnal and secretive. "I feel you, my brother" I tried to bond with the chicken sized creature before me.

He had a long, slender bill which even furthered our similarities. "But don't you worry, my flightless little brother, *my secret* won't be a secret for much longer if I can just get a moment alone with my commanding officer, and not a half-naked man, or a bird," I finished resolutely.

I was reemphasizing my intent to come out of the military and subsequently the closet.

Looking up, I gazed with a twinge of fear at the snow caped mountains before me.

"Did you know that the Kiwi as an emblem first appeared in the late 19th century on New Zealand regimental badges?" I queried my little friend as we began our trek towards an open road, which was a metaphor for my life at this point.

It would take me thirty days to get back to civilization so I could *finally* resign my commission.

Little Kiwi looked up at me, as if to say "Look, Yankee Doodle, you're a real **bloke,** and it would be a **box of budgies** to go on a walkabout with you to **wop-wops,** but I'm going to **bugger off** home before my **sheila** thinks I've got a **spinner** on the side."

I had *yet* to encounter anyone in this country who spoke the Queen's English.

Shortly thereafter I stumbled upon what we in America would call a Ranger Station. However, in New Zealand they are strategically located, fully stocked, and open for use by avid trekkers.

Bounding through the wooden door to this welcome refuge from the glacier cold, I was greeted by two sets of eyes. No, not animals, although close; they belonged to two boys from Australia. With outback enthusiasm they jumped up from two overstuffed chairs, punched me repeatedly on the shoulder and said "G'day, **mate**, **alright**?"

"Someone give me a dictionary *please*," I thought, recovering from the blows.

Later that day, I reentered the cabin having gone outside to spew the **vegemite** sandwich the boys had eagerly made for me. Suddenly, as if they had been hiding somewhere, two Malaysian girls appeared.

Boy, girl, boy, girl I calculated. "Where's mine?" I said jokingly and voila, Ian appeared from behind the door to the **loo**.

He was from Dunedin, and my knees went week at the sight of him; tall, young, handsome, athletic, and he spoke English. "Hi, I'm Ian" he spoke elegantly as if a relative of the Queen while extending his hand gentlemanly.

"William," I replied at a loss for words.

"Look, Will," he continued our dialogue for us, having shortened my name informally, "That door leads to the toilet, which is outside. It's what we in New Zealand call a long drop, which is nothing more than a hole in the ground."

"Thanks, Ian" I said, now able to say more than just one word.

While holding his hand, and striving to make a complete sentence I spurted out "That's a nice sweater." Phew, four words, baby steps, William, baby steps.

"Thanks, or **ta** as we say here," he replied, "I got it at a sheep shearing farm I visited in Rotorua – have you been there yet?" he asked with sincere interest.

"No, but I smelled it," I said honestly, reflecting upon my arrival in Wellington, and wishing immediately I hadn't put it quite so.

The Aussie boys, back in their comfortable chairs by the fire let out a chuckle, while Ian motioned me politely towards the sofa.

There, next to him, I could feel his warmth as he shared more with me about his experience from the sheep shearing farm on the north island. He continued gracefully by comparing it to the sheep grabbing game he had witnessed in Xinjiang, middle kingdom of China.

"Hot *and* educated," I purred to myself as I melted into his story.

"Let's eat," the two Malay girls sang out, interrupting my brief love affair. I glanced towards them fretfully, hoping they wouldn't be serving more vegemite!

That night, the Aussie boys slept in their chairs, arms over the back and feet over the arms. They looked like big, adorable puppies but I restrained from stroking their hair and scratching their bellies. The Malay girls had their own tent, and I was invited to share Ian's tent.

The next day as we finished packing our back packs, we all looked at each other vaguely, waiting for someone to begin the farewells. Without speaking we all just started walking in the same direction. We were now a band of six that would last for the next thirty days.

What had happened the previous night in the tent with me and Ian? Remember, my dears, often it's not what is said, but the unspoken that you must interrupt for yourself.

At the onset of our trek together, we all hiked the challenging glacier, and I was thankful for and boasted about my brand new hiking boots.

This had not gone unnoticed by the Aussies.

Some days later we left the glacier, and entered a plateau that extended for as far as the eye could see. The two Aussie boys took point and lead the rest of us along a river formed by the melting glacier. We trusted their instinct, and followed them obligingly. I had no suspicion of what was about to occur.

Midpoint through the plateau, the leaders did a hard right turn, and entered the river as if intending to cross it. From my vantage point in the middle of the formation still at river's edge, I could see no other route – especially one that would prevent my new boots from getting wet!

There were no rocks in the river to use as stepping stones, and as most glaciers and environs are treeless, I couldn't pull a Tarzan stunt. It was inevitable; my boots were going to get wet.

"God damn it to hell," I belted openly for all to hear.

I followed the leaders, entered the river, and was knee deep in freezing water, my boots wet, of course, when the formation stopped in its tracks.

Everyone looked towards me and applauded. My astonishment was just as they had wished.

The Aussie boys leading the pack did an about face, brushing past me to exit the river and said **"She'll be right**, mate." We continued along our original shoreline course unabated.

I whipped around to face Ian only to find on his face a smile, resting above shrugged shoulders. He coughed with discretion, while glancing towards the two key conspirators. Hot, educated, *and* playful – I was in love for the first time!

I would have my revenge, my pretties I calculated as they all fatigued with the raptures of the event.

The following day, after having finally drying off completely, we continued our trek and descended off the plateau. We now had to use an inflatable raft and do a rapid descent by water over treacherous rapids.

"Ha, boats and water – we're in my element now!" I mumbled under my breath, eyeing my trek mates mischievously.

I took charge of the expedition and provided the inflatable raft. I stationed Ian and myself amidships, the safest part of the vessel. The girls were placed directly in front of us so I could keep both an eye and a rope on them. The Aussie twins were separated; one was sent forward, one was sent aft. The lure of the river was exhilarating.

Once underway, the forward Aussie took the brunt of the splashing waves, while the aft brother got dunked several times much to my delight.

Yet, the piece de resistance would be at the terminal end of our ride, at shark fin split.

Reaching a split in the river, we now had a choice: follow the river to the right of the fin shaped rock formation, where the flow was not as strong, indicating a more gradual descent, or to the left which had a strong flow, indicating a rapid descent.

They all of course chose the right fork, and I yielded to the majority.

Little did they know; I had foreknowledge of this river. My having been deposited on the glacier was not as abrupt or mistaken as I have led you to believe – I chose to go on this thirty day trek before reporting for duty in Christchurch. As such, I had reconnoitered and was well studied on local topography.

"Right fork it is, mates" I chirped with a knowing, ear to ear smile.

We glided calmly for miles, everyone happy in their choice.

Suddenly I began to receive excited reports from both the bow and stern that the river was beginning to narrow dramatically. Tension became palpable as the flow of water increased at an alarming rate as a result of the narrowing river.

"Stop!" pleaded the Malay girls too late to prevent us from being siphoned into a cavern.

I steered the raft forward into darkness. We were at the mercy of the water's flow by now. A few taps of the ore on the granite walls surrounding us prevented impact, but it was obvious who was in control – the river.

Blindness made our skin tingle.

Sunlight suddenly illuminated our horrified faces like a camera flash, and we were propelled out of the cavern and lost all sense of gravity.

The river had turned into a full-fledged, one hundred and eighty degree down, water fall.

Some terrifying moments later, as our heads all bobbed out of the water at the bottom of the falls, it was now my turn to smile and shrug my shoulders at Ian. His beautiful smile in return was full of silent praise. I had successfully completed my mission of revenge, from lure to **loar**.

Some days later after we had dried off, again, we reached civilization.

The city lights of Queenstown twinkled around our band of six, as we meandered through the streets on our last night together.

"What's that squeaking, duck-like sound?" asked one of the Malay girls innocently glancing in my direction.

"The **Yank's** boots!" the Aussie twins laughed in unison.

Ian, ever eager to please me asked "Will; what do you want to do tomorrow, our last day together?"

"Live happily ever after here in New Zealand with you," I said openly for the first time in my life to another man, and in earshot of other human beings.

Notwithstanding that fantasy, I suggested another love of mine: ships. "Let's take a day cruise on the *TSS Earnslaw* on Lake Wakatipu," I said softly to him, while looking at the two Aussies with a challenge in my eyes. A majority of us girls decided in my favor.

Standing dockside the next morning **when the sparrow farts**, even the **Aussie-ockers** were in awe of the ship's turn of the century elegance. She was a 1912 Edwardian vintage twin screw steamer, and was named after Mount Earnslaw, a 2889 meter peak at the head of Lake Wakatipu.

She was designed to be the biggest boat on the lake at forty eight meters long.

When construction was finally completed in Dunedin she was dismantled. All the quarter inch steel hull plates were numbered for reconstruction much like a jig-saw puzzle. Then the boat parts were railed by goods train across the South Island from Dunedin to Kingston at the southern end of Lake Wakatipu.

Six months later, after being rebuilt, on 24 February 1912, the TSS Earnslaw was launched and fired up for her maiden voyage to Queenstown.

Underway, we watched as the stokers fueled the original fire boxes, and felt the welcome heat from the boilers. From the strength of her steam engines in her belly, she belted out an operatic note on her whistle announcing that "The Lady of The Lake" was at Court.

After lunch, we for once agreed unanimously *not* to join the sing-along around the piano. For my part, I wasn't getting anywhere near a piano least

I be enlisted to play it. We all walked aft in stride towards the relative seclusion of the poop deck.

Whilst we all leaned on the railing in reflection, the girls suggested that we each tell a story about something memorable in our lives.

The snow caped mountains in the distance from whence we had come now framed Lake Wakatipu before us, as we each pondered the question.

The Aussie boys readily chirped about getting drunk in Sydney, then spewing all over Bondi Beach. The part worth remembering was, according to their testimony, beach goers the following days lying in their puke.

Bondi, by the way, is a favorite outdoor venue in Australia for Americans!

The Malay girls said in polite form that they had yet to experience their memorable experience, a trip to America. This was spoken over loud guffaws from the Aussies.

Ian looked at me directly, as if his response was for me only, and said the last four weeks were the best of his life.

The Malay girls smiled...the Aussie boys now had muted guffaws, either from their admiration for the fact that I had gotten my revenge earlier that week for my ruined hiking boots, or sheer ignorance to what had actually been taking place between Ian and myself.

I looked away from the mountains, and slowly down towards the deep blue water. After a few moments, without even looking up at my audience I began my most memorable story.

"In deep blue water, much like this, the battleship *USS Iowa* (BB 61) is conducting gunnery practice near Puerto Rico," I recited flatly.

"Almost nine hundred feet long, and fifteen stories tall the *Iowa* is one of the biggest and most powerful ships ever built," I informed them with pride. "It is also the only Navy vessel ever with a bath-tub, a feature installed for Roosevelt when he was shuttled to the Middle East in 1943," I added lightly.

"Storing and handling large quantities of highly explosive gunpowder had been a challenge since dreadnaughts were first built – and even more so now, as the young crew of the *Iowa* was using gunpowder bales from the 1950's," I continued with concealed emotion.

"A gun turret on a battleship is, in your terms, about the size of a small, two storied ranch house," I informed my listeners with a sideways glance. "Each turret has within it, three long cannons, shall we say," I finished in layman's terms, returning my gaze towards the water.

"Gun turret one fires its first round of split salvos, using 2700 pound shells, propelled by six, forty five pound silk bags of gunpowder. The center and right gun fired normally, but the left gun misfired.

A second round of shells and powder are loaded, and the left gun misfires again," I continued.

"The breech door to the left gun is closed, and will remain so for two hours, a full one and a half hours more than regulation, before inspecting the gun," I recited it all evenly seemingly without taking a breath.

Stopping now to look in the eyes of my enthralled listeners I struggled to continue. "However, that incident had no bearing on the tragedy that was about to befall turret two," I stuttered with foreboding.

"Orders are given to turret two to commence firing," I started my story again, now with unconcealed emotion and looking nowhere in particular.

"The breeches for the two outer guns are closed and locked within seventeen and forty four seconds respectively of the order to fire. They are elevated to their firing position," I pause to conceal a tear, my eyes rising slowly towards the sky.

"Left and right guns are loaded, good job boys," sings out GMCS Reginald Ziegler, "but the center gun is having a little trouble."

"I have a problem here, I am not ready yet," radios GMG3 Richard Lawrence.

Senior Chief Ziegler shouts to LTJG Robert Buch "Tell plot we are not ready yet, there is a problem with the center gun!"

Gunners Mate Third Class Lawrence repeats himself with annoyance "I'm not ready yet, I'm not ready yet."

Seconds later an unidentified voice screams "Oh my..."

I look down from the clouds, and my eyes are now full of tears as I struggle to finish.

"The breech of the center gun had not been closed, and the rammer was still in the barrel when smoke, unspent powder, flames and hot gasses burst out of the open breech. The gasses swept through the lower turret substructure and erupted through the three gun ports, the vent ducts, and rangefinder hoods. The gun bloomers were ripped from the turret's faceplate and blown away from all three gun ports. Thick, hot, gray smoke billowed forth, scorching the teak deck beneath what remained of turret two, its lifeless carcass now pointing to starboard, guns askew. Forty seven men were now dead," I stopped abruptly.

The Malay girls were a mass of tears.

Ian had his arms loosely around me.

Even the Aussie boys proved they had a soft side when they said gently "You right mate? **Fair dinkum**!"

"**Too right**, mates; **dinky di**," I agreed, having regained control of myself and in the four weeks we had spent together learned a new language - Australian.

Now that we were all of an understanding, I fired my own salvo testifying "And yet, the Navy Investigating Service would concoct a lame excuse about a gay love affair gone awry, and that the turret had been sabotaged."

"Trust me, mates," I spoke directly to the jury of five on the deck of the *TSS Earnslaw*, "I personally know what it's like to be the brunt of an investigation by the Navy!"

"At least I was alive to defend myself," I concluded firmly.

"And one day, when it's safe for me to be 'out' I'll summon the courage to tell how two *straight* young men wrongfully got the blame for the disaster on the *USS Iowa*."

"**Good on ya**, mate" whispered Ian, his arms around me now forming a firm embrace.

I Told You So

CHAPTER THREE: ESPIONAGE

Christchurch, New Zealand: population four hundred and eighty one thousand heterosexual men and women. "And now, just one openly homosexual man," I speculated while feeling clearly obscure.

Well, I was almost *open* and *out*.

I had finally made it to base, and completed my last mission – to resign with honor.

My resignation from active military duty had been accepted in less than dramatic, yet efficient military fashion by the base clerk. Forms were filled out, documents signed, more forms, more signatures.

"A signature reveals a man's character," I said boldly to the uncaring clerk. "Sometimes even his name if written legibly," I mumbled with a smile and a half glance in his direction, then down at his questionable handwriting. I left the office with a bounce in my step.

By voluntarily leaving the service I so dearly loved, my head held high, I was in control of my destiny and was effectively telling the military to "Kiss my gay..."

Only days thereafter, I was greeted by my Commanding Officer with unusual warmth. I was told in an oddly sympathetic voice that headquarters had decided to postpone my discharge until I had served my full two years in New Zealand. It supposedly had something to do with the logistics of getting a replacement for me on such short notice, in this remote location.

For some unknown reason I trusted the skipper. I couldn't quite put my finger on why we got along so well instantly, and decided not to dwell on it. Instead, I would hunker down, do my duty, and be all that I could be for the Navy (apologies to my Army friends for borrowing your motto).

I rented a house in Riccarton, a suburb due west of Christchurch city center, separated from it by Hagely Park. It is where most well to do Europeans had first settled, and where most Americans now stationed in the country chose to live.

Automobiles brought into New Zealand have hideous import taxes levied on them, which explained why most folks, even Riccartonites, drove seemingly antique cars; the exception being the Americans, who if stationed here were exempt from the import fees. They could bring in brand new Mercedes, BMW's, Jaguars and so forth for a *fraction* of the price a Kiwi would have to pay.

But wait, there's more to this injustice: after two years, the Americans could sell the cars on the open market, at market prices which included inflated values due to the taxes, and all without paying the taxes!

Their profiteering made me sick, as did the lifestyle we lived in the wealthy suburbs. Our American wages were two to one above the **kiwi** wage, due to the currency rate differences.

I quickly moved, and refused to participate in the automobile scam. I rented a modest top floor **flat** on *the other side* of Hagely Park where mere mortals lived in town, and bought a twenty five year old, British racing green Triumph Spitfire.

I had visited a gentleman who was remodeling his house, and wanted his spare car out of his garage. Opening the garage doors, the low profile, soft-top, rumbling roadster spoke to me. I started it up and drove it around the block. It was the first time I had ever driven a Spitfire, and the feeling was both exhilarating and unforgettable.

She continued our dialogue through her dual exhaust, and gave me a sense of freedom with her top down. When traffic signals changed in our favor, she pushed me back into the seat with her acceleration, and we were gone and alone together again!

This choice of car endeared me hugely with my New Zealand civilian staff on base, all who responded at the sight of her by whispering admiringly "**sweet as**!" American eyebrows on base were raised suspiciously in my direction – but still, not the skipper's.

However, the Spitfire almost cost me my life, as early one Sunday morning, when the sparrow farts, I went for a drive and discovered at the last minute that I was driving on the wrong side of the road.

My little two door baby saved me by quickly getting things right – I mean left!

One week-end while driving in the countryside towards rural Nelson, I passed a sheep farm and instantly welled up with tears as it reminded me of Ian who I missed tremendously.

I renewed my vows to be free, regardless of the fact that I was *still* active duty military.

I would have one **boondocker** in the military, but allow one stiletto to peak out of the closet – simultaneously, if not figuratively.

"I hope I don't trip and fall with this mismatched footwear," I cautioned myself.

But just how does one find other gay men in Christchurch? Are there any? Where are they? What will they look like? What do I do if I find one?

There being no military instruction manual on the subject, I would have to reconnoiter on my own.

"What does one wear for such a mission?" I drilled myself, "Khaki, camouflage, white for summer, black for winter – shit, even those last two familiarities are ass backwards down here as the seasons are reversed in the southern hemisphere!"

Santa coming in the middle of summer, and me going to the beach in the middle of December would only add to the utter and total confusion I was feeling during this time in my life.

"Winter is summer and summer is ..." I stirred myself into an excited frenzy.

Hey, give me a break. It was my first gay mission.

"Perhaps if I listen to Vivaldi's *Four Seasons*, I'll calm down and sort things out," I reasoned with myself. His music will give structure to my life, and be a check list and compass.

While opera ties music closely to words, instrumental music at best reflects an abstract overall mood.

However, with the *Four Seasons* Vivaldi decisively bridged that gap. Each of the four concertos is prefaced by a sonnet (presumably written by the composer) full of allusions ripe for sonic depiction.

Summer brings torrid heat, buzzing insects and a violent storm.

Yet, the thunderous noise the residents of Christchurch were about to hear would not be reason to grab a **brollie**.

During the weeks I was deciding what I would wear to my first gay bar, and summoning the courage to actually go through with the reconnoiter fact finding mission, I had bought a Harley.

I loved my afternoon and week-end trips on it to Brighton Beach in the summer, in December, where the atmosphere was a bit more, *relaxed* shall we say?

"Torrid heat?" I queried myself while examining my check list; check.

"Buzzing insects?" I further examined my manual to the seasons while squashing a bug with the check list itself; check.

"Violent storm too?" you ask in anticipation. That would be the noise from the nervous churning in my stomach, because I was about to engage the enemy; check.

Strolling through the quaint shops that dotted this beach town, I found the second hand book store I had heard of. Once inside, out of the corner of my eye I noted a curtain towards the back of the shop with a hand written sign above it that read "adult."

With cunning and stealth I approached the target area, and then committed to full penetration.

"Mission accomplished," I rewarded myself under my breath once inside, while feeling more fear than I ever had felt even on a real combat mission.

My new surroundings were more foreign to me than any of the over 50 countries I had previously visited, invited or not.

One thing within these environs made my heart literally stop as surely as if a bullet had gone through it – a gay magazine. My hand trembled more when reaching for this magazine, than it had done holding the magazine for an M16 riffle in training.

Mind you, I had held a gay magazine before, in small remote towns in America on my getaways in my Mercedes, and where no one knew me from the preacher's son. However, this county, this town, was small, smaller, and smallest and I was the only one in the book store who didn't speak Kiwi. It was a certain tip-off to my enemy presence, I cautioned myself.

So, I did what I had been trained to do by the military; snatch and grab.

The objective now was to retrieve the intel and then leave as quickly as possible.

Indeed, leaving this back room unnoticed presented varying number of enemies appearing in the distance. These enemies included an elderly woman in the cooking section, and the front desk clerk. Both could have been easily taken down from my vantage point using a sniper rifle.

Too messy, I surmised while continuing to survey the battlefield.

Then I spied the solution to my exit strategy – a Newsweek magazine.

Concealing the gay intel inside the Newsweek, I approached the clerk. His singular, unwavering gaze at me over the top of his glasses was a challenge to revel my gathered intel, I was sure.

"I may have to abort," I decided in a flash until I heard him say levelly "four dollars, fifty – ta."

I exited the battlefield and ran faster than I had done in Nicaragua where my life had actually depended on it.

Retrieving my extraction vehicle, I raced on my Harley back to my flat in Christchurch unaware of mere traffic laws, barely able to contain myself.

Safely at home base, in the back of this glossy magazine whose pictures were of no interest to me, well, maybe some interest being human after all, I found the information I had been seeking: a directory to gay venues in Christchurch.

"I deserve a medal for this mission," I commended myself sitting back exhausted, eyeing the eight military ribbons, and three military medals I had earned during a lifetime of service. They were now in a frame and adorned the corner of my desk, not ignominiously.

Resolve is never stronger than in the morning after the night it was never weaker.

Chapter Four: How to Repair Closet Doors

Even with my gathered intel, it would be some time before my brain would acknowledge and carry out orders from my heart.

"No matter how far in or out of the closet you are, you still have a next step," I instructed myself while wandering the streets of Christchurch keeping an eye out for signs of gay life.

One autumn day, in March, I was walking down the main drag called Hereford Street, towards what would later become my second home – The Gym — when suddenly I was drawn into a tucked away piano shop.

Upon entering, I was immediately summoned to the very rear of the shop, past the proliferation of new Japanese and Korean pianos, by a nine foot long, concert grand John Broadwood piano.

John Broadwood & Sons is the oldest and one of the most prestigious piano companies in the world. The instruments have been enjoyed by such famous people as Mozart, Haydn, Chopin, Beethoven and Liszt - and William Bonzo.

The company holds the Royal Warrant as manufacturer of pianos to Queen Elizabeth II.

In August 1817 Thomas Broadwood, one of John's sons, met Beethoven in Vienna, and later recalled, "he was kind enough to play to me but he was near total deaf and unwell."

In 1818 Thomas Broadwood wrote to Beethoven, offering him a piano. Beethoven wrote back in February, "I shall regard it as an altar upon which I will place the choicest offerings of my mind to the Divine Apollo."

One wonders how it survived the journey after being shipped to Trieste in the spring and taken to Vienna by mule and cart over mountain passes and roads no better than rough tracks.

He became very appreciative of the rare six-octave grand given him, preferring also the bigger tone of the English piano.

The piano still exists in the National Museum of Hungary in Budapest.

The store clerk in Christchurch eyed me suspiciously, since I was obviously of a lesser class than Haydn, Chopin and so forth. Ignoring his scrutiny, I accepted the call of the piano, sat down, began to play and melted on the spot.

The strong metal plates used in building the piano give it a heaviness of touch but a fullness of vocal resonance to the tone. The piano and I were one, as surely as Ian and I had been. While I had previously played for audiences of uniformed sailors, I now had an audience of only one civilian who viewed me as scurrilous.

I felt the clerk's gaze change quickly from suspicion to amazement. He raised a finger, and opened his mouth in preparation to speak. I interrupted him abruptly saying "Never interrupt someone doing what you thought couldn't be done – Amelia Earhart."

He froze on the spot.

"Homosexuality is god's way of insuring that the truly gifted aren't burdened with children – William Bonzo," I uttered evenly yet in full voice in response to his rigid form, without even looking up from the piano. I had been playing Vivaldi's autumn, which celebrates me, the peasant.

"How will you get it up and into your top floor flat near Hagley Park?" queried the clerk without looking up from the bountiful harvest of cash I had placed on his counter after my visit to the bank.

I hired a crane.

Yep, a full-fledged, three legged, five story tall transforming monster that took up half of my building's lawn, and half of Park Terrace Avenue to the degree it required police assistance to re-direct traffic around Godzilla.

All this was necessary, as the only way to get the nine foot long piano into my flat, in a building without a **lift**, was through my living room window, which yes, we had to remove, casement and all.

Was I crazy? That's what the New Zealand Herald said, but I was American, so was excused. Furthermore, it didn't take much to make headlines in Christchurch – a fact I was now keenly if not cautiously aware of.

When the crane left the premises hours later, one of its paws had left an eight inch deep impression on my building's lawn. The property owner was not happy, until I suggested it resembled a Kiwi's foot, and we could make it a flower bed for next spring's block gardening contest.

I loved going to the gym, I loved my piano; now where were all the gay men?

"Why is it that, as a culture, we are more comfortable seeing men holding guns than holding hands?" I asked myself half-heartedly, losing interest in that battle as I lovingly brushed my hands over the ivory keys on my new baby.

"Ironic, isn't it, that the military will give you a medal for killing men, but a discharge for loving them," I mused while making my way through the now familiar Hereford Street towards The Gym.

The Gym was full of men, but to date I was neither trained, nor fully qualified to use **Gaydar**. Sure, many of us exchanged glances, even stares, but I hadn't gotten fully acclimated to the nuance of the language in New Zealand – Māori or English.

I simply had to stop being such a wimp, take the initiative and go one night to an out and out, in your face, openly gay bar.

76 Lichfield Street: that was the address gathered from my intel.

I imagined neon signs, colorful banners, and men dripping with men near the entrance and got excited at the thought of it all. I jumped on my Harley and went with bated breath to meet my destiny.

"Hey, **Pakeha**, who's that **bloke** who keeps circling the block on his motorcycle?" said the Māori patron of Angles Nightclub to the Englishman patron as they stood together looking with puzzlement out the third floor window of 76 Lichfield Street.

Apparently, all there was to indicate I had arrived (after circling the block for an hour) were two simple, three inch tall numbers "76" on a paint peeled door frame.

Parking my Harley right in front of the door, removing my helmet revealing short, military length blond hair, and removing my cycle jacket that had been struggling to cover my muscled chest and arms, I glanced up and imagined I saw the curtains in the third floor window fly shut, and heard someone scream then hit the floor with a thud.

"Lord, lead me not to temptation; I found the way myself," I said under my breath as I put first my left foot, then my right foot in front of me with far less certainty then I had done during cadence at boot camp.

"Yes sir, the angels are sleeping but the devil has left the light on tonight," I continued with increased courage as I reached the precipice of 76 Lichfield Street and looked up, and towards the glow from the windows.

Climbing the wooden stairs, I felt and heard ever increasing thumping sounds. "Was everyone dropping dead up there from a gas leak, or was it the beat of the music?" I shouted over the loud beats of my heart.

A door man who wore all black and resembled Lurch from the Adams Family greeted me at the summit of the stairs with two words "Members only."

My heart stopped beating.

I was quickly revived by one of the peeping Toms who had left his passed out partner on the floor near the window in order to greet me at the door.

"I'll vouch for him," said my new best friend excitedly while putting his little hands as far around my bicep as he could and struggled to pull me in – to the club.

My openly gay life had officially begun.

What did it look like inside the club? Hey, "Members only." Perhaps I'll vouch for you later.

By spring, in August, I would not only be a member but I would come to be one of the most popular bartenders, both during the club's business hours and "after hours" throughout the remainder of my two year tour of duty in New Zealand.

In further preparation for the prestigious block gardening contest, and heralding my new found gay identity, I planted all pink petunias in the rear of the building where I lived. They were positioned proudly near my unit's entrance, and were in the shape of a triangle. The front of the building had a kiwi's foot planter. Our block won! More scintillating headlines ensued.

Now the challenge was not to be in the military and hide that I was gay, but to survive what little time was left of my military career while being openly gay. I would struggle to keep a rein on the years of pent up frustration and emotion that had been pounding on the inside of the closet door, yearning to be free.

However, my proverbial closet door had not only opened, but seemed to have been blown off its hinges and was lying on the carpenter's pile.

The pendulum had swung and I was trying to hang on.

I felt the motion of the ocean, yet was on dry land.

Free at last, free at last; thank Liz Taylor almighty, I was free at last!

But, we'll have to get back to all that because for now I had been summoned to see the Admiral! My heart stopped again.

Yet know this: Resolve is never stronger than in the morning after the night it was never weaker. Resolve became my adrenalin.

I Told You So

Chapter Five: The Admiral Wants to See You

"Good morning, skipper," I said rather cheerfully, a new sense of freedom in my voice, "What can I do for you?" I finished while surveying his perfectly kept office.

His hair was also well coifed at all times, and his manner refined – yee gods, was I developing gaydar? That would mean he was...

"Admiral Jones is in town for a week, and you're to be his escort," he replied with soft, even tones. "What's more, the Ambassador is sending his car and driver down from Wellington to pick up that special something you have for him," he concluded politely and looked me directly in the eyes for an unusual, yet comfortable length of time.

"Well, when you're popular," I said with a mock Royal swirl of my right hand into the air.

"Put your hand down you wanker," I chided myself. "Fresh out of the closet and already you're morphing into a bloody **poofter**," I finished my self-repudiation, hoping the skipper hadn't noticed.

"This could be the hardest mission of my life; trying to appear normal during the day and, well you know, being the other thing during the night," I forecast.

"Now, William, you probably think this is a lot..." he began.

"Don't go and accuse me of thinking," I interrupted him with a smile.

I was dismissed politely.

After a crisp salute, I did a regulation about face, nearly tripping over my own feet as I noticed out of the corner of my eye a plaque on the wall behind the skipper which read "Be who you are and say what you feel, because those who mind don't matter and those who matter don't mind." ~Dr. Seuss.

Exiting the building and slipping on my uniform cap, I walked into the still brisk, yet sunny Christchurch weather. I half-heartedly looked left and right to locate the base Infirmary, because I was sure my brain needed re-wiring due to all the mixed messages I had just gotten.

I was in as much of a spin, as was the joker I had met at Angles last night who spit at me from his drunken stupor "Bisexuality is a blessing and a curse, but viewing it as a schizophrenic will make you insane."

I was only sure of one thing from the meeting with the skipper; I had to stroke both the Admiral and the

Ambassador at the same time. "Just one of those serendipitous moments in life," I muttered in the air.

Bright as a button I entered my office at the base Exchange/Commissary and told my secretary "Please bring me the Ambassador's ketchup."

"Will his car and driver be picking it up, as usual?" she asked matter of factually.

"Yes, ta Jackie," I replied politely. Civilians in New Zealand were much easier to get along with than civilians I had supervised in New York. In fact, just about everything in New Zealand appealed to me more than any other place I had been in the world.

"A country of inveterate, backwoods, thick-headed, egotistic philistines" Vladimir Ilyich Lenin had said of New Zealand.

"No disrespect, Vlad," I shook my now uncovered head in polite disagreement while rubbing my hair to remove the crease my uniform hat had made, "but I love everything about this country - except their **tomato sauce**." It was their version of a condiment we in America call ketchup.

While this country had innumerable assets, it lacked certain delicacies the American palette was accustomed to. For that reason, twice a year I ordered and received a cargo container full of American food.

The Ambassador must have had a shipping directory in his office in Wellington, because no sooner than the ship had secured its mooring lines in Lyttelton harbor, his car was on its way to Christchurch.

Yet on this day, and out of the ordinary, the Ambassador's driver appeared in front of me with another urgent request - orange juice! Apparently there was a party for dignitaries the next evening at the Consulate in Wellington, and he needed Florida fresh OJ, ASAP.

"What do you think this is, Safeway?" I said to him with mock anger while matter of factually handing Jackie the requisition form with a polite smile.

"Let's grab a beer, while we wait," he suggested eagerly.

Walking towards the base canteen, I was half tempted to tell him "I like my beers cold and my homosexuals flaming hot."

Actually, I didn't like beer at all until Ian had introduced me in Queenstown to a drink called The Depth Charge.

"Is this in reference to my being in the Navy?" I had asked him, reaching for the stein glass.

"You'll see, after you go *down on it*," Ian had replied with a twinkle in his eyes.

It is a large stein glass of beer, usually Lager, with a shot of Drambuie dropped into it, shot glass and all. You drink the beer, all the while the Drambuie seeping out of the shot glass slowly until ka-boom!

The bulk of the Drambuie hits you glass and all like a depth charge.

"Don't drink and drive," I said to the taillights of the Ambassador's car as it left base, only to have another official vehicle approach me face on with headlights aglow – it was now the Admiral.

"If society is anti-gay, does being gay make me anti-social?" I pondered as the Admiral's car came to a halt in front of me. "I need a social secretary and calendar at this rate," I continued with myself until interrupted.

"Hello, Bill," beamed the Admiral in an overly friendly tone, "Anna sends her regards."

"G-great!" I stuttered awkwardly in reply, having almost successfully forgotten her – until now. "How's your wife?" I queried politely, recovering composure.

"I haven't spoken to her in years – I don't want to interrupt her," he quipped.

I remembered the awkward dinner at their mansion in Newport, thinking "I spent a year in that house – all in one Sunday!"

"Look, Bill, I want to buy some sheep skin rugs and woolen sweaters," he continued his informal posture, "Can you help me with that, Bill?"

"Absolutely, sir" I chirped with military perfunctory.

"Thanks, Bill" he exuberated while continuing to pump my hand.

"You call me *Bill* one more time, *Mac*, and I'll *Bob* your ears" I kept to myself, preferring to be called William, or Will. Instead I responded with "Sir, I could have had them shipped to you, and saved you the twelve thousand mile trip."

"No problem, Bill, I needed to use some of my travel budget, and I've heard great things about you down here in New Zealand," he said proudly.

"Like what, my successful reconnoiter mission that led to the discovery of a gay bar?" I wondered.

"Sir," I began again out loud, "Do you know that if Fedex and UPS merged, they would be FED-UP?"

"What's more, stupidity is not a handicap, so could you park your car in a regular spot?" I continued silently.

His cheerful façade began to show cracks, and I'm sure the kettle had started to boil so I offered respectfully "I know just the place, sir."

I lead him to an entire wing of my Navy Exchange that was devoted solely to sheep skin rugs, a popular favorite for servicemen and women who passed through Christchurch going to, and from Antarctica.

"This is not what I had in mind, Bill" he said firmly, stopping suddenly in his tracks four steps behind my lead.

I turned towards his position and said to myself "Honey, this aint Marshall Fields."

"What did you have in mind, sir?" I said out loud, politely.

"Let's go *shopping*!" he belted out.

"You go girl," I mumbled safely under my breath as he had already retreated towards his car still parked in the handicapped stall.

The shops of Christchurch awaited our invasion.

"Do you know what the most prevalent vocation is for gay people in New Zealand?" I asked and answered myself as the Admiral diverted his stride into my office, "Shop Attendant."

What's more, efficient gay gossip channels had already been busy at work disseminating information about the American GI Joe who works at 76 Lichfield Street.

He had tucked quickly into my office to change clothes, and emerged ready to shop. "Whatever look you were going for, sir, you missed" I said out of the corner of my mouth to Jackie who sat at her desk and pretended to be using the typewriter.

I kept pace behind him and used my hand to cover my mouth as I coughed, and muttered "Nice cologne, sir, must you marinate in it?"

"What was that, Bill?" he asked rhetorically from the back of his head without breaking his reinvigorated stride towards his car, intent on shopping.

"Night alone..." I repeated for clarity, "...you can suffocate in it." I was pointing north animatedly, using my story of my arrival in New Zealand and the overwhelming sulfur smell as an explanation for any misunderstanding.

We entered every shop in town, and every shop attendant winked at me and blew me kisses. The Admiral said nothing. Perhaps he was just jealous they were winking at me.

Shop, after shop, after SHOP – I was ready to drop, and I'm gay; we're supposed to shop!

"Why is it that Americans can't make the right decision, until they've tried all the wrong ones?" I queried the first attendant who we had already visited hours before.

He gave me a pinch on the ass, which I brushed off with a half glare, half smile. "Call me," I whispered to him, pinky and thumb imitating a phone held to my mouth and ear.

Now, the admiral wanted to do lunch and he blew me out of the water when he said "I like natural foods, do you Bill?"

Yet without missing a beat I fired my own salvo saying "I used to eat a lot of *natural* foods, until I learned that most people die of *natural* causes."

Equally unstopped he added "My wife gave me some health books to read..."

"Be careful of reading health books," I interrupted him, "You may die of a misprint!"

Sitting together at a small café, he took on that relaxed, far away, reflective look that tourists often acquire after just one day in a foreign country - in addition to shopping bags full of cheap souvenirs.

Or was he contemplating my court-marshal and imprisonment for me being such a wise-ass, and gay?

Personally, my contentedness came from having learned of the country in the months I had lived here.

"Sir, did you know that the first European to find New Zealand was a Dutch sea-captain who was looking for something else?" I asked almost rhetorically as he had now given his full attention to lunch and his head was buried in the menu.

Turning my attention away from the overly friendly waiter whose smile was afforded to me alone, I continued speaking to the Admiral's forehead "It takes its name from a province of Holland to which it does not bear the remotest likeness, and is usually regarded as the antipodes of England, but is not."

The Admiral spoke his lunch order towards the waiter without even looking up from his menu lest he should miss some gastronomical delight, while the waiter continued his unspoken, yet overt gestures towards me.

"It was subsequently taken possession of by an English navigator, whose action was afterwards reversed by his country's rulers," I persisted in what was becoming a surreal montage, "and it was only annexed by the English Government which did not want it, to keep it from the French who did."

"When George Bernard Shaw visited New Zealand a reporter asked him his impression of the place and, after a pause, Shaw is said to have replied: 'Altogether too many sheep'" our waiter added to the confusion.

The Admiral remained nose deep in his menu, either from indecision, or an escape from the flurry of words that were buzzing around our table, and that were worthy of a Woody Allen script.

Un-thwarted by my pursed lips, furrowed brow and proceed at your own risk stare, our waiter continued innocently "Robert Muldoon said that New Zealand was colonized initially by those Australians who had the initiative to escape."

Wanting to bring the Admiral back into the conversation, I waved a hand across the sky, perilously and intentionally close to the waiter's face, and spoke with mock sincerity "I can see the headlines now, as the Admiral returns to America and is asked to comment on his trip to New Zealand and responds with: Terrible tragedy in the South Seas. Three million people trapped alive."

His belly laugh shook the wine glasses on our table and he seemed at ease. I assumed, hopefully, that the waiter's flirtations had gone unnoticed, as well as those of every shop assistant we had encountered earlier. Or had they?

"Are you married yet, Bill?" he queried me out loud, followed quickly with the same question by the waiter – silently with only an incredulous eye popping, jaw dropping look in my direction.

"Yes," I replied first to the admiral, "I was married by a judge…" Turning my gaze towards the waiter I finished my response with "…but I should have asked for a jury!"

The waiter disappeared in a huff at my tease. I'm sure I heard a tray drop, and breaking dinnerware. I muffled a laugh, and desperately attempted to turn it into a believable cough, replete with hand over my mouth, a quick widening of my eye lids, and a slight after cough.

Alone with me, the Admiral leaned in close and shared "My wife has a slight impediment in her speech - every now and then she stops to breath."

Right! Does one laugh at the joke? Or was he being serious, and confiding in me?

"Waiter: two Irish Coffees!" I shouted towards the bar, buying me some time to consider my response, and future.

"Irish coffee provides in a single glass all four essential food groups: alcohol, caffeine, sugar and fat," I spoke flatly to the Admiral in mock support of his new healthy living bent.

On our drive back to base, our car was overflowing with sheep skin rugs, woolen sweaters, and other purchases. I was both physically and mentally exhausted!

With what remained of my wits, I was daring myself to suggest the admiral have a tee-shirt made as a souvenir of his trip to New Zealand. It could read VENI, VEDI, VISA: I came, I saw, I charged it!

We had only spent a day together, yet it seemed like a week. Deja-vu?

"And that's my report on the Admiral's visit," I concluded to the skipper a week later at quarters, letting out a huge sigh of relief.

He reached behind himself, towards a book shelf underneath the Dr. Seuss quote, and quickly selected a well-worn title.

Placing it on his desk for me, he quoted from it without even turning the cover: "I believe we were all glad to leave New Zealand. It is not a pleasant place. Amongst the natives there is absent that charming simplicity.... and the greater part of the English are the very refuse of society, Charles Darwin 1860."

"Perhaps if Mr. Darwin, and certain others, had spent more time here, his opinion would have 'evolved' as have yours and mine," the skipper spoke softly and directly towards me.

That brief moment of intimacy was followed simply by "you're dismissed."

I sat down with a thud, into my oversized leather desk chair in my office at the Navy Exchange. My ribbons, medals, and letters of commendation adorned the wall behind me like artwork at the Louvre.

"Every child is an artist. The problem is how to remain an artist once he grows up," Pablo Picasso had once said. "OK," I began my retort, "then where does the portrait of my life go from here?" It seemed rather abstract.

I was staring blankly out of my office window, my gaze going right over the runways choked with C130's on their way off the ice, and back to the United States. I was taken all the way to Mount Cook when Jackie interrupted me gently with "Lieutenant?"

"Jackie, please?" I chided her softly, "Call me William."

"No worries, Lieutenant" she responded with her kiwi accent that always warmed me.

"Until I was thirteen, I thought my name was SHUT UP!" I shared with her. "What's more," I continued an intimate revelation with her, "I'm sure I'm adopted because I don't look at all like my parents, or my siblings."

"Perhaps you're the milk man's son, then?" she said still in character, if not a bit staccato for emphasis.

With a rewarding laugh, I turned from the outdoors and asked her what I could do for her.

"I need your approval for the off-season protocols," she said evenly, placing a folder on my desk and brining me back to work.

CHAPTER SIX: PRISON

Some weeks later, the summer tourist season was over in New Zealand. The Admiral and others had gone – and it was February.

At the precipice of the Navy Exchange I ducked instinctively as an outward bound jet flew overhead a little bit too close.

"Did you feel that one?" asked Jackie, noticing the startled look on my face as I entered the office.

"I was walking from the skipper's office to here, and the stewardess told me to sit down during take-off" I responded with disingenuous candor.

We had both poked our heads outside to check the plane's final trajectory, when I pleaded into the increasing chilly air "Vivaldi, I could still use a little help here." I was still genuinely confused by the seasons in the Southern Hemisphere.

"Autumn is a harvest, celebration, and a hunt," I recited out loud, now satisfied that the plane hadn't indeed crashed, and I could return to my personal dilemma.

Jackie and I lingered for a moment in the door way of the Exchange/Commissary surveying a now strangely empty base. Without changing my forward gaze, I asked Jackie "Why do they call it tourist *season*, if you can't shoot them?"

She chuckled in agreement, placed her hand softly on my arm and directed me into the building saying "Let's go Mr. B, we have inventory to do and next *season* to prepare for."

"Nonsense," I yelled out, releasing her grip on me and rising to full posture, "Tell Wally to get the van, and gather the staff at once."

She went to gather the staff as ordered, while I stood in my office and said with full theatrics for all to hear, "This isn't an office, it's Hell with fluorescent lighting -let's escape from this prison!"

Moments later faithful Wally whisked the van to a halt in front of the Exchange.

"How did you get it from the motor pool so quickly?" I asked with a puzzled look.

"One carton of cigarettes, and one case of beer," he replied sheepishly.

"You were robbed," I spoke down to him, "It usually only takes a carton of cigarettes!"

The van soon was full with my bewildered staff eyeing each other for a clue as to where we were going. The Exchange/Commissary was void of life and locked tight. I commanded to my trusted Māori employee Wally behind the wheel, "Mush!"

Everyone knew Jackie was my right hand so leaned towards her and whispered, "Jackie, has he lost it?"

"Define *it*," she said less to them than to me.

Having heard their whispers from my command post in the front seat I responded to them all "I plead contemporary insanity." Turning to see the impact of my words, I saw bewildered faces on all except Jackie. She was only bemused, as she alone understood my impulsiveness, among *other things*…

We were going on a pique-nique.

Driving south east from town, we travelled along the Summit Road which provided breathtaking views of Christchurch and the Banks Peninsula. Our final destination would be Mt Vernon Park, a good place to explore the easier slopes of the Port Hills. I didn't want to kill anyone with a strenuous glacier hike, much of my staff being older than Methuselah.

The Port Hills are one of the best-loved landscapes of Christchurch. The tussock grasslands and rugged rock out-crops, contrast the flatness of the Canterbury Plains. Remnants of a **podocarp** forest are reminders of the past.

We parked at a spot on a gentle slope. My now eager and increasingly playful staff began arranging lunch from the treasures I had hidden earlier in the **boot** of the van.

I walked forward, slowly approaching Jackie who was leaning back gently against the van's **bonnet** with her arms across her chest in a relaxed manner. She was looking peacefully over the horizon when I ungraciously interrupted her. Holding a spatula and pan I queried "I have a hankering, do you want fries with that?"

Having interrupted her quiet moment earned me a tightly pursed sneer, and a half lidded glare, followed by Shakespearian quality undulating eyebrows and rippling vocalism in response to my tease. Yet it was all in good fun, as she didn't have a mean bone in her body.

"Why is there an expiration date on *sour* cream?" I asked my crew as we sorted through the food on our blankets laid on the grass.

Wally, having secured the van and perimeter in military fashion joined the fun with "If you ate pasta and antipasti, would you still be hungry?"

"I'm not sure, Wally," I continued the banter while unpacking the wine basket, "Personally, I cook with wine, and sometimes I even add it to the food."

"I distrust camels, and anyone else who can go for a week without a drink," added Jackie while opening with a pop a bottle of **Canterbury's** finest.

Through quiet observation, it had become aware to me since I first arrived on base that I was not the only one with a special relationship with

Jackie. The skipper and she were seen often in the canteen, talking and laughing over glasses of Merlot.

Laughter all around, the view, and a break from base made for a memorable day by all.

Sated, we lingered. The day was **good as gold**.

"Now and then it's good to pause in our pursuit of happiness," I spoke calmly into the air, "and just be happy."

Back on base the skipper met us at the gate, as we returned with travel fatigue worthy of a Norman Rockwell painting. He looked straight at me through the passenger side, front open window and said "I see the Exchange/Commissary was closed today."

"Inventory, sir," I responded perfunctorily while trying to brush the remnants of our debauchery under the van seat with my foot. Standing fast in my mock deception he turned quietly to Jackie, who reassured him with only a slight tilt of her head that all was well.

Orders done for our next shipment of OJ and ketchup, sheep safe on their farms until the next onslaught of tourists, and most personnel off "The Ice" until next "season" I took a week of leave to visit Ian in Dunedin.

He lived in the second largest city on the south island of New Zealand. Considering Christchurch is nearly the smallest city in the world, to me, it didn't bode well about its size. But, size didn't matter to me because I'd be with Ian.

As I drove through the **Waitaki** district where the city is located, I was awestruck by its haunting natural beauty. Whitestone architecture punctuated rolling green pastures.

These hills surrounded a long, natural harbor, which had attracted Māori settlers to the site over four centuries ago. Subsequently the area was settled by whalers, gold miners and migrants principally from Scotland.

On the doorstep of the city, I found incredible wildlife including the world's rarest penguins, a mainland albatross colony, fur seals and sea lions. Within the city, I found Ian.

We had lunch at once, since I was famished. Remembering my dislike of vegemite sandwiches he prepared instead for me, in his modest flat, tomato and cucumber sandwiches. As he approached the table where I had been waiting, and admiring the view, *of him preparing lunch*, I said matter of factually "Did you know that tomatoes and cucumbers are considered fruits?"

He placed the sandwich platter on the table with a thud, grabbed me by the hand, pulled me up and close to him, and whispered in my ear with his warm breath "so are you!" Lunch would have to wait a bit longer...

We didn't emerge from his flat until the next morning, when we hired a horse drawn carriage and took the slow route to one of his favorite places – Larnach Castle.

With panoramic views of Dunedin, Otago Harbour, the Peninsula and the Pacific Ocean, the Castle has had many uses: as a lunatic asylum, a hospital for shell-shocked soldiers, and a nuns retreat. The Ballroom was once even used as a sheep holding pen! For our visit, it had been restored to its original glory.

Wandering through its magnificent, formal interior I noticed of all things, a painting of a penguin. "Perhaps in reference to our stone's throw from Antarctica," I mused.

"Ian, did you know that a penguin only has sex twice a year?" I queried him while touching his hand to get his attention.

He grasped my hand firmly, leading me away from the painting and said firmly "You wouldn't look good in a Tux."

Next we passed a full set of gleaming Knight's armor. Now it was his turn to be playfully smart. "Did you know, William, that armored knights raised their visors to identify themselves when they rode past their king, and that this custom has become the modern military salute?" he said smugly.

I responded by placing my free hand to my temple and saying with mock formality "My Lord."

The final room we toured was astounding in that its painted ceiling reminded me of the Sistine Chapel. While looking up I took one last jab at Ian before going outside with him, and said with mock sincerity, "If Michelangelo had not been gay, the Sistine Chapel would have simply been wallpapered."

He couldn't control his laughter, but stopped my silly chatter with a kiss.

We were both painting intuitively, on the canvas of life.

We continued our walk hand in hand around the grounds. I had once said that Eagle Lake, Ontario Canada was heaven. That being true, then I must have died and been reincarnated because this place, this time, this man was heaven.

And while for the first time in my life I had what I wanted more than anything, a man to love, I was also becoming aware that It's not what New Zealanders have that's important to their quality of life - it's what they don't have!

New Zealand doesn't have high crime rates, the NZ police don't carry guns and instances of corruption are virtually unheard of.

There's no abject poverty or hunger, pollution, congestion, health issues or cramped city living that can be seen elsewhere in the world.

The further I was enveloped by this idyllic life, the farther I was from the US Military.

I Told You So

CHAPTER SEVEN: A PLANE IS DOWN ON THE ICE

Ian and I were walking back to his flat in the brisk, autumn evening air of Dunedin, having just seen a film. It was a year since we first met, and half way through my two years of remaining active military duty.

During intermission, we had had a commonality in New Zealand film theatres, ice cream – no popcorn in this country!

Nonetheless, we barely noticed the cold as we were holding each other close both in the theatre with our frozen treat, and as we walked outside afterwards. We discussed the "new release" we had just seen, which had already been in, and out of the theatres in America for months.

We paused at a street vendor for a New Zealand delicacy – fish and **chips** served in a rolled up newspaper. Normally I don't eat seafood, but covered with layers of flour and deep fried grease I didn't know the difference between the fish and the chips. Perhaps, it's true that love makes you blind.

"Did you hear the one about the Scottish drag queen?" he asked playfully, leaning close into me.

"No, my Lord, but I beg, do tell," I continued in character.

"He wore pants!" Ian delivered his punch line, which earned him a punch to his stomach.

"Are you Scottish too, like ninety nine percent of this town?" I asked him inquisitively between mouthfuls of something fried.

"No," he said firmly, "I'm British."

"A country's boundaries are only a matter of dates," I reminded him.

"And you?" he asked while he licked his fingers alluringly making me insane.

"My family is from Switzerland, although when they left the country it was occupied by the French," I informed him.

"So you're full of holes, like Swiss cheese?" he retorted with a punch of his own to my stomach.

"Let's go inventory them," I shouted, my warm breath visible in the cold air, "before we both get arrested for public domestic violence!" I pulled on his hand and we began running through the streets of Dunedin towards his flat.

Sometime later that night, as we lie asleep together, curled up in each other's arms, the phone rang next to the bed. Ian answered it, without even opening his eyes, or rising more than six inches. He then fell back into his comfortable perch beside me, mistook his bearing, range and distance from me, and slammed the phone square in the middle of my face saying "it's for you, sweetheart."

Rubbing the pain out of my nose, I spoke into the handset "Yes...yes...yes."

"One of your Christchurch **bog-queens** looking to hook up?" he mumbled, while pinching me in the side.

One of our National Science Foundation's LC-130 aircraft had crashed on the ice in Antarctica.

Before I could even get back to Christchurch, members of my staff had begun preparing immediately to bring the Navy Exchange/Commissary to full operation again. They acted from experience on short notice to accommodate what was expected to be a sudden and prolonged influx of military personnel.

As they had worked at the base for years before I arrived, they knew what to expect. They acted on their instinct, which I respected. Therefore, when I got back to base I didn't start barking orders; I simply said "What can I do to help you?"

As we prepared for the worst, Jackie reminded me of a previous crash. It had occurred twelve hundred kilometers from McMurdo Station.

That LC130 had gone down hard- two crewmembers had been lost. *It* had been bringing in spare parts for yet *another* of our planes that earlier had been damaged during takeoff.

In general, the Lockheed C-130 Hercules is a highly reliable aircraft. However, conditions in Antarctica can be brutal to both man and even the finest built machine.

After evaluating the situation the National Science Foundation and the Navy made plans to recover the two downed aircraft during the next season, leaving them preserved in the ice for the winter, rather than risk yet another plane down on the ice.

Preparations had been made during the off-season to accomplish the repairs, which meant the base in Christchurch had been full-on over the winter months. After temperatures had risen sufficiently the recovery operations began the next November, the seasons in New Zealand being reversed from the Northern Hemisphere.

This involved replacement of the wing on the first aircraft and of the nose landing gear on the second aircraft.

Jackie finished her story, and brought me back to the present catastrophe with "It could be busy here soon, so put on your running shoes, Princess."

"Lieutenant, I'm sorry for interrupting your vacation," the skipper said to me in an uncharacteristically formal tone, having appeared at the entrance to the shuttered Exchange/Commissary.

My staff, being aware of his presence had taken up position behind me, awaiting any news on the severity of the current plane crash, and loss of life.

"I appreciate the entire staff coming in on such sudden notice," he continued while looking past me towards knowing nods, "However, you can all stand down," he concluded looking at me squarely again. He turned, and then began to walk towards his office.

They all routinely, and without question, began once again to return to off-season protocols.

I however trotted after the skipper, and slowing to keep one pace behind him queried "Captain, that's it?"

"Yes, William," he responded having paused to face me and to choose his words.

He continued evenly, yet with a lighter tone he seemed to use only with me "The Foundation and the Navy have decided to declare this one a total loss," he paused, looking down at the ground searching for the words to continue.

"Perhaps they'll decide to dig this one up sometime in the future, just like the crash of '71 that took fifteen years to recover," he finished looking up with a half-smile.

He patted me on the arm gently, and then continued his walk alone.

I didn't dwell. I was all too familiar with keeping secrets in the Navy.

My personal secret, though, seemed to have quite a few leaks!

"Sweetheart," Ian had said to me knowing full well it was the base that had called.

"Princess" Jackie had referred to me as, knowing full well I am a Prince!

"Still, it shouldn't matter what I do in the bedroom, so long as I didn't do it in the streets and frighten the horses," I reasoned passionately, if not irrationally with myself.

"My own belief is that there is hardly *anyone* whose sexual life, if it were broadcast, would *not* fill the world at large with surprise and horror," said W. Somerset Maugham.

"He must have lived in Utah," I continued the debate with myself.

With the base on official stand down, again, and one day of my vacation remaining, I decided to play tourist in Christchurch.

I had made a friend at The Gym named Aidan, and although we had agreed we were both gay, I had agreed he wasn't my type. This being at least partially understood, our friendship grew. He now agreed to meet me on my last day of vacation, where else but at Cathedral Square and to play tour guide.

Arriving at the square late the next morning, I was greeted by an odd figure in a long black robe, a tall pointed black hat, and white beard that held a crooked staff. "Aidan?" I whispered to the apparition before me.

"Here, mate," I heard from behind. "That's The Wizard of Christchurch, our national icon," Aidan said informatively, and with affected pride.

Looking again at the now identified "all seeing and all-knowing" one in the middle of the square, he had climbed to the top of his wooden ladder and begun his performance to the delight of the assembled crowd.

"In certain trying circumstances, urgent circumstances, desperate circumstances, profanity furnishes a relief denied even to prayer," proclaimed The Wizard, quoting Mark Twain.

"At no time is freedom of speech more precious than when a man hits his thumb with a hammer," I responded boldly to him, earning a knowing nod of his pointed black hat in my direction.

"Truth is, mate," continued Aidan, "he served in the Royal Air Force as a pilot-officer navigator." He faced me and challenged me for a response.

"Ah, a navigator, that explains it," I said with a shrug, motioning Aidan towards a small café I noticed out of the corner of my eye.

Strolling towards our lunch venue, I recited to Aidan the story of my "navigator" cell mate from boot camp.

We arrived shortly at 96 Hereford Street for lunch.

The simplicity of venue nomenclature in New Zealand continued to amaze, if not leave me wanting.

Greeting us at the door was a woman, of equal uniqueness to that of The Wizard, who said cheerfully "Table for two, *eh?*"

I was being
called “dad.”

CHAPTER EIGHT: THE CANADIAN CONSPIRACY

96 Hereford Street, Drexel's Restaurant would become my fourth home, after Angles nightclub, The Gym and Ian's bedroom in Dunedin.

It was owned and operated by Canadians Norm and Julie Drexel, while the waitress was a perky young **sheila** who also overused the word "**eh**."

To Aidan, they were an oddity to be taken casually. To me, they seemed like cousins, and while I was at once at ease with them, there was something I couldn't quite put my finger on...

My curiosity about them would have to go on the back burner, as the food arrived at our table. Aidan and I were presented with, well food fit for the Gods.

We couldn't contain ourselves. We abandoned our manners, in favor of the shovel method of eating often used by officers aboard ship.

"This is *not* fast food," I dropped an oxymoron on Aidan.

"Fast food?" shouted our server with disdain. "That would be the equivalent to pornography, nutritionally speaking and this is a respectable establishment," she finished our repudiation while returning to the kitchen, turning slightly to offer us a smile.

"Too right," Ian quipped in response while dabbing a napkin to his eye, "there's a lot more juice in this grapefruit, *than meets the eye*."

Acknowledging his well-played line, I served back with "In the military, the menu consists of two choices; Take it, or leave it."

While the food was going rapidly into the front of my face, inside the back of my head an argument was taking place.

"The cuisine of the western provinces of Canada is heavily influenced by Italian, British, Ukrainian, Polish, and Scandinavian cuisine" the right side of my brain told me. The left side of my brain said "shut up and eat."

"The Ontario region has a tradition of Mennonite and Germanic cookery resembling what we are eating now," the right side persisted.

Aidan interrupted us asking "Who are you talking to mate?"

Even Norm and Julie had begun to look cautiously in my direction.

I returned their gaze with equal suspicion, and a fixed gaze of my own, gently touching in succession each corner of my mouth with the napkin indicating I was done for now, but that this wasn't over!

Near the exit my interest in this venue, this couple Norm and Julie, was peeked when I read above the door: "All happiness depends on a leisurely breakfast" ~John Gunther.

"Much more investigation of this restaurant is required," I told my lunch companion with an impolite, deep throated burp.

Aidan now guided me towards Park Terrace Avenue, a stone's throw from Drexels, knowing full well that my flat was located there.

Reaching that precipice I diverted our direction towards the Avon River and away from my flat. I suggested firmly "Let's walk off lunch."

Unbeknownst to us at the time, the banks of the Avon River, directly in front of my flat, would in the not too distant future be the sight of yet another news-worthy event of my doing. It would be even more spectacular, and far surpass the mundane piano moving, and garden events that played out sometime before. Tour buses full of tourists would roll to a halt, camera shutters would be clicking to capture a glimpse of...

For now, all was peaceful this afternoon on the banks of the river, which meandered through and around the largest open urban space in Christchurch, New Zealand – Hagley Park.

The park had been at the heart of Christchurch sine the 1850's. "It offers a diverse range of entertainment and recreational facilities," I read to Aidan from a free brochure I had picked up from a kiosk.

"Diverse? You aint seen *nothing* yet," I forecast, having already been formulating party plans for my *final* release date from the United States of America military, and the stranglehold they had had on most of my adult life.

"I wonder if there are enough queens in New Zealand to fill all of the park's 165 hectares (407 acres)?" I asked myself, already preparing the guest list in my head.

"Do the boys still live with you?" Aidan asked with affected casualness as two young men from the University of Canterbury passed us, his eyes following them with no compunction whatsoever. They looked dapper in their school uniforms, on the preferred method of transport in this town – bicycles.

"Yes," I replied succinctly.

"You know," I continued without missing a beat, "I was accepted to the University of Canterbury, MBA program. It would allow me to stay in New Zealand a couple more years, but I wouldn't be allowed to work, legally."

"What's more," I shared with my disinterested listener, "I am certain they only accepted me as their token American, and that I would inevitably fail – educational standards here being so much higher than in America."

Now I asked him with similar affected casualness, "Why does everyone in Christchurch ride a bike? I see people on their way to school, to work, to church, even to the shops and they're all on bikes!"

The question was correctly interpreted by Aidan as rhetorical and went unanswered.

Having failed thus far to divert his attention from my sixteen, and eighteen year old wards, I further suggested we pick up the pace and run the fitness course, "And get you away from my boys," I mumbled under my breath.

"Ta," he replied less than enthusiastically, and *walked* in the opposite direction.

During my solo run, I encountered many other joggers, walkers, and tourists out enjoying the various sights and activities that made the park such an important part of Christchurch.

At my flat, my boys were *just* waking up!

Madison, my eighteen year old was in his boxer shorts and one of my military tee shirts. He was playing my nine foot Broadwood grand piano as usual.

His younger brother, Taylor was only sixteen and was standing in his bedroom doorway, stretching his small, shirtless five foot tall frame in mock attempt to touch the ceiling when I entered the flat.

"Hi, dad," he said smiling and lowering one of his arms to greet me with a hand placed gently on my shoulder.

"Mom's coming for dinner tonight," said Madison without turning from his favorite position on the piano bench in the living room, which faced Hagely Park.

"Yee gods," I sighed looking towards Madison, while catching Taylor off guard with my back-handed slap to his washboard flat stomach.

"I wonder if Drexel's will deliver?" I asked myself out loud aiming now towards the kitchen to do inventory – two growing boys can eat you out of house and home.

And this had indeed become their de-facto home since having been thrown out of their maternal home by the very person who now had the temerity to invite herself to dinner!

The two brothers had appeared one night at Angles, suddenly homeless. Their mother, upon learning that they were both gay, had in her Christian charity said "Get out of my house!"

The age of consent, or when one is considered an adult in New Zealand is sixteen.

Having taken pity on them, I offered my spare bedroom for the night. Before you could say **"Bob's your uncle"** my flat was theirs and I was being called "dad."

Brushing past me en-route to the kitchen, Taylor said with more wisdom for his years than should be expected "I'll cook, dad. You can just go polish your sword."

I gave him a quick glance, wanting to know which *sword* he was referring to.

From the shower, I could hear Madison had switched his repertoire to one of my favorites, The Four Seasons by Vivaldi.

"You're spot on, playing winter," I raised my voice over the piano, the sound of pots and pans in the kitchen, and the water running. With their mother coming, I expected an early frost.

At least she was punctual, arriving at the appointed hour. I was certain I saw frost on my pink petunias, if not in her eyes as I opened the door for her.

Taylor continued preparations in the kitchen, and I cowardly joined him there offering to help. Madison, the older of the two brothers assumed role as host and showed their mother the flat. This was her first visit since the boys had come to live with me.

The meal was superb, the atmosphere was worrisome.

"Eat," I commanded softly to my boys, "Worries go down better with soup – Jewish proverb."

Without even looking up from his soup, Taylor said bravely "The only thing more exasperating than a mother who can cook and won't, is a mother who can't cook and will."

Looking sheepishly at me for my response, I met Taylor's eyes with mine, which were full of silent applause.

"Quite so, my boy, quite so," I nodded while continuing to enjoy the delicious meal.

"A gourmet who thinks of calories, is like a tart who looks at her watch," I added while their mother fumbled with her time piece.

Madison, from the wisdom of his years over Taylor and I combined, played referee by offering "He who distinguishes the true savor of his food can never be a glutton; he who does not cannot be otherwise ~Henry David Thoreau."

Audible applause erupted from me and my youngest son now both sitting fully erect. To be sure though, it was just polite taps of the right hand fingertips onto the palm of the left hand – this is New Zealand after all, and not the exuberant American colonies.

After an insufferable amount of time, dinner was finally over. Madison and Taylor both cleared the dining room table, disappeared into the kitchen behind a two-way swinging door that had curiously stopped swinging the moment after they had passed through it.

They had left me on the battlefront, alone, with the enemy -their mother.

For another eternity, she preached at me the evils of homosexuality.

"You want to joust?" I asked her, silently. I put my left hand behind my back, raised my sword in my right hand, figuratively, and did battle with the enemy. I always kept my friends close, and my enemies closer and as such, had a thorough knowledge of the Christian Bible.

My real, Navy Officer's sword though was only a few feet away on the fireplace mantle, I calculated.

I started with Genesis 1:31 "God saw all that he had made, and it was very good."

"If He doesn't like gays, why does he keep making them?" I asked evenly.

"Being gay is a choice," she interrupted me.

"Right," I fired back, "just like skin color?"

"Thou shalt not lie with mankind, as with womankind: it is abomination, Leviticus 18:22," she shot a broadside.

"The same book condemns wearing clothing of more than one kind of fiber, planting more than one kind of crop in the same field, and eating shrimp," I returned the volley of fire, rubbing my fingers on her blouse sleeve to check for fiber content, and eying the table where she had devoured Taylor's masterpiece – shrimp scampi, "Quote one, quote 'em all, I say."

My opponent being weakened, I attacked using her own weapon, the Christian Bible. "Passages in 1rst Samuel and 2nd Samuel describe, among other events, an extremely close bond between David and Jonathan," I paused to explain that

Jonathan was the son of King Saul, and next in line for the throne. "Don't you find it inconceivable that God would allow a famous king of Israel to engage in same-gender sexual activity?" I asked her incredulously.

Notwithstanding her inevitable retort about choice and free will granted by God, I stood my ground and offered 1rst Samuel 18:2 "From that day, Saul kept David with him and did not let him return to his father's house."

"So, David left his parent's home and moved to Saul's where he would be with Jonathan. This is a strong indication that the relationship was extremely close. What's more it echoes the marriage passage in Genesis 2:24: Therefore shall a man leave his father and his mother, and shall cleave unto his wife, and they shall be one flesh," I concluded my sermon to stunned parishioners which included the two sets of eyes peering form the gap in the kitchen door.

The battle ended in a draw as discussions of this sort must; this because, in the end, it is a matter of one's beliefs. Beliefs which themselves may embody sharing them with the world, but which mustn't entail *forcing* them on others with different beliefs.

Now, should one wish to convert one's beliefs, there indeed is the free will that God, whomever you believe Him to be, is manifested.

I assumed the role of a British Gentleman, offered her my hand with a slight bow, and said firmly "Let me show you out."

When we reached the door to the flat, which was adjacent to my open bedroom door, she flung me around to face her closely, tugged fruitlessly on my two hundred pound frame, struggling to pull it towards my bedroom, motioned towards the bed with her head and said with an undulating voice "Five minutes in there, and I'll make a man out of you."

Her religious garb, of questionable fiber content, had fallen off her frame faster than she had hoped to undress and convert me.

"Good evening, madam" I continued my role as gentleman, standing upright with a forward fixed gaze until the entrance door to the flat was shut behind her.

"*Boys*" I said firmly, doing a crisp about face and marched towards the door that separated the dining room from the kitchen.

It had now closed the final inch, and as I approached it I heard laughing as the alternate escape route, a door between the kitchen and living room was pressed into use. After a mock chase through the flat, they surrendered and I held one in each of my arms, joining in the laughter.

"Santa Claus has the right idea," I began my summation of the evening, "Visit peoples homes only once a year!"

"Can I have the car tomorrow to go to Brighton Beach," asked Madison between laughs, assuming I wouldn't recognize his tactics.

Emboldened, Taylor chirped "Can I go to Cathedral Square tonight with my friends, dad?"

"You've both got a **bloody cheek**," I replied through pursed lips, and squeezed them tighter, holding them close.

I loved them both, unconditionally.

CHAPTER NINE: INTERMISSION

Two years had passed since I first set foot on the tarmac in Wellington, two years I had been made to wait for my final release from active military duty.

There was only one duty I had left to the United States Military: I would walk off base honorably, my head held high, one final salute.

Subsequently I obtained a one year travel visa, and during that one year I remained in New Zealand and would live an *entire* lifetime I had previously been denied.

No man or woman had loved their country more than I had, nor served it with greater pride. Now it was time to love myself – *and serve every man in town!*

This place is on fire tonight!

I Told You So

Chapter Ten: Turn up the Music!

The intermingled smells of smoke and sweat and too many people instantly assaulted the nostrils of two more members who had been cleared by the doorman at Angles night club, 76 Lichfield Street. The two flamboyant boys pushed their way through the pulsating throng, inhaled deeply and proclaimed "Ah, it's good to be home."

"It may be winter outside, but it's hot, hot, hot in here," said Lurch guarding the entrance, causing me to drop a case of beer. His unusual verbosity startled me.

"Too right, this place is on fire tonight," I delighted.

The broken bottles of beer only added to the aroma.

The nearest snow was on top of Mount Cook, which meant the stomping sound in my ears wasn't from frozen feet. Everyone had forgotten their cares outside, and was inside to dance!

Thump, thump, thump, thump thundered the bass speakers, challenging all to fill the dance floor. La da da dee da da da da, La da da dee da da da da came the second challenge to any one silly enough to be remaining on the sidelines as La Bouche belted out "Be my lover."

"Until the end of time, won't you be mine" one boy lip-synched the song lyrics indiscriminately to all the other boys now filling the dance floor.

"Or until the clock strikes morning," I shouted at the other bartender from our vantage point behind the bar and just next to the dance floor. We watched heads bob up and down, bodies swing to and fro, and listened to the chatter.

At this relatively early time in my openly gay life, I was temperamentally untrained to realize the glow of celebrity. Instead I marveled more at the sexual politics. There was no more thrilling nightlife in Christchurch than 76 Lichfield Street, and I asked myself "How long can the Gods allow this to last?"

Suddenly, a pretty young thing landed at my bar and I thought "You won't be pretty or young forever but oh, what stories you will have to tell."

"Gin...and Tonic" he mouthed gasping for breath.

As I handed him his drink, he nodded and melted away, vanishing into a sea of humanity.

From a musical standpoint, Angles night club did not seek to break new ground, but rather to feed its patrons a familiar diet of dance hits.

Without missing a beat the music switched into Dancing Queen, and I was forced, willingly, to dance. Now it was my turn to lip-sync "Dancing Queen, young and sweet, only sevent... something," I stumbled on the words.

I felt a pair of hands on my waist just then, and jumped at the sensation. Turning quickly, my eyes locked with Ian's. There were no words that could sum up the intense wave of emotion as I looked at my man. My skin bristled at his touch, the small blond hairs on my arms raised, despite the heat, and the fact that I had felt his touch a thousand times before.

Just as soon as I had felt him, he was gone, dancing off into the throng, smiling and touching a dozen other men casually while looking in my direction for my reaction.

"I'll get you, my pretty," I shouted over the music and took up pursuit.

The dancing lasted throughout the night, in open violation of City ordinance.

The next morning, it spilled from Lichfield Street, down Hereford Street past Drexel's Restaurant, and curiously ended up on the banks of the Avon River – directly in front of my flat.

Unbeknownst to me, it was my freedom from the military party.

My boys Madison and Taylor had prepared for our arrival by placing four enormous speakers at each open window of our flat. When the entourage from Angles arrived at Park Terrace, the two masterminds pushed play on the music box and turned up the volume.

"It's astounding, time is fleeting, madness takes its toll..." began the sound track to Rocky Horror, a popular favorite in New Zealand.

In no time I was stripped to my undershorts by Madison, painted gold head to toe by Taylor and thrust into the middle of the chorus line as the star – Rocky.

We all began to move in unison to "It's a jump to the left, and then a step to the right, with your hands on your hips..."

What a bunch of Queens, and I loved them all! I glanced towards my flat, and the two I loved the most, only to see them motioning with theatrical emphasis towards the right end of the street.

"Oh shit," I shouted unheard over the beat of the music and chorus of voices as I caught sight of three approaching buses that slowed to a halt in front of us.

"Are they prison busses, come to take us all away?" shouted an anonymous voice with careless enthusiasm from the midst of the unruly crowd.

"No mate," I replied towards everyone, "They're just tourists and we're the zoo monkeys!"

The flash of cameras competed with the oncoming flash of police car lights that had joined the melee from the left. News media at every turn only stirred the frenzy.

Eventually the tour buses moved on, their occupants no doubt wishing they could have joined us.

The media had had their fill *for at least a month*.

The polite police officers corralled us off of public property and onto my side of the street. New Zealand was an especially tolerant society.

I mounted the balcony of my flat, surveyed the crowd surrounding my building like a Queen, raised my hands into the air and proclaimed, "On with the dance, let joy be unconfined!"

"Kiss him, kiss him" the crowd shouted enthusiastically back towards the balcony as Ian had taken his place beside me. We acquiesced to our subject's demands, to their great delight.

According to the New Zealand Herald, the party ended about a month later.

Having escaped the arm of the law, I exited the shower in my flat where a pool of gold was swirling counter clockwise down the drain. I reached for Taylor's arm that held a towel, when Madison said from his usual perch at the piano, "Can I have the car again?"

"Madison has a boyfriend, Madison has a boyfriend," Taylor giggled as he turned towards the kitchen to make us all tea. I caught him with a snap on his cute little ass with the tip of my wet towel, just before he was out of range.

I reached my bedroom, and smiled down at Ian as he was napping. His dark eyelashes rested lightly on his cheeks and his chest rose and fell gently. I ran my fingers through his hair hoping not to wake him. It's was getting longer now and I loved it. It fell beautifully around his face and looked amazing when paired with that bright beautiful smile he was so well known for. I kissed one of his eyelids, then the other and smiled again as he smacked his lips and grinned a little in his sleep. I settled in and rested my head on his bare chest, falling asleep to the steady beat of his heart.

I was the first to wake up after our nap, and of course did one of my favorite things in the world; I watched Ian sleep. The sun was coming in through the crack in the drapes of our bedroom, casting a beam of light onto Ian's face, lighting his features, making him look positively angelic. I wondered where he had hidden his wings and halo. I pushed the hair away from his forehead gently and at that moment, his eyes fluttered open and he gave me a soft smile.

"Hey," he said his voice scratchy from sleep.

"Gi 'day," I said looking down at him lovingly.

We neither of us really knew what to say...the day was too perfect to be wasted on frivolous conversation. We settled for snuggling up to each other, and I put my head on his bare chest again. Ian put an arm around my neck, hugging me close to his body. We heard the bed room door open, but didn't bother to move to see who it was.

"Awww...how perfect," Taylor purred.

I just smiled and kissed the top of Ian's head.

Taylor came in with a tray full of food and placed it on the bed squarely in between me and Ian.

"Madison and I figured we wouldn't bother you both, and would let you have your tea in here," snapped my youngest as he did a pirouette and exited with mock jealousy.

"Sounds good," I said paternally to the back of the bedroom door.

As we ate we exchanged small talk and just enjoyed the quiet time that was so rare with two boys in the house. Ian giggled at the look on my face after he had leaned over and stolen a strawberry from my waffle.

Madison and Taylor liked to see Ian and I like this, having fun, and not being so wrapped up in the dual life I had previously been living, or my new struggle; immigrating to New Zealand.

I Told You So

CHAPTER ELEVEN: REVELATION

The very next night after the mother of all parties we were all back at good old 76 Lichfield Street.

I was behind the worn, black wood bar dressed, or rather undressed, to kill. My arms and chest that had first earned me entry to this private club were covered only by thin black straps of leather.

To my left, Madison was snuggled into a quiet corner of the front lounge, in one of the several overstuffed chairs. His arms were around his new boyfriend – a real stunner! At the window, the two peeping Toms were keeping vigil for any new comers who might be unaware of our members only status, and yet worthy of entry.

To my right, Taylor was dancing nonstop, uninhibited and shirtless, the little tart.

To be sure, while our charter was for a "Social Club" the dance floor was at the heart of Angles Night Club. We had no dress code, nor was there any drug sub-culture as in many American and European clubs.

At the rear of the club were rows of stack chairs for the wall flowers - Aidan was as usual on the hunt. These chairs could be removed, and often were, when none could resist the call of the music. In this event, Aidan would move his lair to the corner of the bar near the entry.

Ian had taken a train home to Dunedin.

Kiwi's drink a lot of mixed drinks that use milk, and we had run out. "I'm going downstairs, mate to borrow some milk – back in a tic," I shouted over the music to the other bartender.

He nodded without even a glance at me, as he was busy preparing multiple drinks at once for the usual hoards of princes and princesses.

"Do keep an eye on Taylor, won't you mate?" I spoke directly into his ear before leaving the bar area, "ta." In just two years in New Zealand, I had without realizing it myself, lost my American accent.

He tilted his head slightly towards me and nodded knowingly, then did a quick visual survey of the club in order to reconnoiter Aidan's position.

Downstairs was a very popular Italian restaurant on the second floor of this three story building. Their patrons weren't necessarily gay, but it was no secret that a gay nightclub occupied the third floor. Each separate venue was keenly aware of the other, but in the fashion of an advanced society, we tolerated each other, albeit at times with furtive glances or down right gawking.

As the building had no dedicated service entrances, other than the front doors of each venue, in order to borrow the milk I needed in the third floor club, I was forced to walk right through the second floor restaurant, from entrance to kitchen, for all to see.

Needless to say, not every citizen in Christchurch had seen a muscle-body in leather before, although they may have wished to. "That," said my inner voice "would be motive enough to have dinner here, and not elsewhere, eh?"

Having walked the runway, I arrived at the kitchen. Head cook neither asked what I wanted, nor looked up from his leg of lamb preparations. He routinely motioned me with a quick nod of his head towards the chill box.

"Ta," I responded perfunctorily and helped myself to the milk, while pausing for a moment to observe cook's method.

"No worries mate," he chirped, still more interested in his lamb legs than mine!

"Did you borrow some **L & P** soda water earlier, before we opened?" he queried evenly while changing from leg of lamb to lamb stew preparation.

"No mate, but I did take some **bangers** and **crisps** for the bar, cheers," I replied.

"How did you get in, mate?" he asked without taking an eye off his stew, "The doors were locked and the alarm set."

"Puleeese, I'm Sicilian!" I pretended in mock defense with Mafioso hand gestures, which earned me a laugh but still not eye contact.

"Time for a **cuppa**?" he said placing the kettle on the fire, and looking at me for the first time, now that his preparations were sorted.

"Cheers," I thanked him, "I should **naff off** and keep an eye on my sons."

"Good on ya mate," he patted my arm, me worried that he was eyeing it for a roast.

Back through the two-way kitchen doors and through the crowded restaurant I went. I was thinking more about Taylor upstairs, than I was about who might be down here. The gaggle of Kiwi accents had become familiar to me, and simply contributed to the din of noise that was another busy night in the building.

I was thinking that Aidan was upstairs trying to "**give his ferret a run**," so I picked up my pace through the restaurant, in order to resume protective duty of my boys.

Suddenly I was stopped dead in my tracks by one, sole, American voice – It was my commanding officer!

I resembled a deer in the headlights and was shocked senseless. What's more, I was half naked and my skimpy leather attire and black eyeliner didn't indicate that I was here for dinner with the skipper.

He began the dialogue, speaking in American, by saying "William, what are you doing here?"

Waiting for my reply, he performed a lingering appraisal of my attire with his eyes.

As my life passed before my eyes, I slowed the film to review frame by frame all the incidents the skipper had given me reason to pause when I was on base with him.

The clues added up, and suddenly it was as if cook had hit the projector in my head with a fry-pan, started the film again, and I had a revelation.

I turned to face him directly, grasping my milk bottle but *not* through infancy, and responded firmly in Kiwi, subtitled here in American "Sir, what are *you* doing here?"

His continued hold of my eyes, and his broad smile with a slight tilt of the head forward, told me all: I was in fact, now fully qualified to operate gaydar!

I also became fully aware of how I had survived two years of active duty, while having one foot still in the military, and the other out of the closet. He had turned a blind eye, to among other things, my having been referred to as sweetheart by Ian, and Princess by Jackie in full earshot.

With mutual, half salutes to our uncovered heads, we parted. I went back to my freedom, and he went back to his dual life that I was all too familiar with.

Sometime later, I would learn that he retired from active duty, managed to get his immigration visa, and settled into a quiet life in Christchurch.

Returning to my realm at Angles, I deposited the bottle of milk on the edge of the bar, nearly dropping it on the floor. My full attention was given to locating the whereabouts of my two boys. Madison was old enough to look out for himself, a trait I admired, yet Taylor was still of an age. I had only been downstairs for moments, but it seemed like a fortnight away from them.

Back behind the bar, I replayed the scene that had taken place in the restaurant to the other bartender, as we continued to serve up all the pretties before us. "Mate, he could have had your **guts for garters**!" he yelled at me over the beat of the music.

"**Hooray**," yelled one of our patrons as he walked away from the bar. If I didn't know that it meant "good by" in Kiwi, I might have been offended.

He was replaced in front of me by a sweaty Taylor, who between breaths, and sucking face with some young stranger, managed to say "Hi dad, **G&T**, ta."

I presented him with an **L&P** instead, and he was not exactly a **box of budgies**. Grabbing his **fizzy** by the bottle and **floozy** by the arm, he spun around and just before he was enveloped by the crowd I heard him say "Love you, dad."

"He **looks flash**," shouted the other bartender which earned him a knock down punch from me.

"Would you two like to be alone?" asked a thirsty patron having eyed the rough physical exchange.

"Good on ya," added his mate.

"What would you two **hard cases** like, before you naff off?" I asked firmly having separated myself from the other bartender.

"**Struth**?" they asked, "We just want to touch your arms."

"**Crikey**," I laughed so loud it carried across the dance floor.

I placed both elbows on the bar, flexed for them, and both their jaws dropped to their **Wellies**.

I glanced towards the dance floor and caught Taylor, keeping a watchful eye on *me*! We exchanged broad smiles, and then I was brought back to the bar when the two **randy poofters** asked boldly while fondling the goods "Do you do **take-aways**?"

As we were closing down the club that night, while cleaning the alcohol soaked bar my thoughts turned to my skipper.

"Mate, give us a hand with this, ta" said my coworker as he motioned towards the **dust-bin** full of empty bottles, trying to bring me back to the present.

"Do you know," I continued with unswerving thought as we struggled down the stairs, "If my skipper, or any Yank for that matter, had come up here last night it would have been as if they had entered a foreign-film?" I reflected on my first night in this private club.

"Yea, mate," he began his response as the subtitle writer tries to keep up, "Too many Kiwis, let alone Yanks, and Angles is **up the boohai shooting pukeko's with a long-handled shovel.**"

I'll baptize
it, and you!

I Told You So

CHAPTER TWELVE: BORN AGAIN

It's September, and spring in New Zealand.

I'm listening to Vivaldi's *Four Seasons*, and imagine I hear a profusion of birds, the breath of gentle breezes, a murmuring stream, swaying plants, a goatherd lulled to sleep and shepherds holding a celebratory bagpipe dance.

Waking up, Ian is lying next to me in a field of green that is now the Port Hills of Christchurch. "Did you hear bagpipes?" I query him.

He destroys all my illusions by responding "I heard you snoring, so I whispered in your ear, poured some L & P, shook you to wake you, sang you a song, and then whistled loudly in your ear."

His alternate yet parallel version of my dream was disturbing.

"What do you want for your birthday?" he asked sweetly.

A Rolls Royce passed by us at that moment, yet I said "Dinner at home with you and the boys."

Reaching into my shorts pocket, he snatched the keys to my Spitfire and proclaimed "I'm driving."

"What?" I defended my driving habits, "It's been years since I drove on the wrong side of the road."

"Yes," he informed me, "but even though it takes thousands of bolts to assemble a car, it only takes one nut to destroy it."

We made for the car with mock urgency. I stood by her and patted her bonnet while eyeing a Toyota in the next parking spot. I continued my defense with "What's more, if I did crash into another vehicle, Japanese tin is no match for my British steel!"

"Hi dad," chirped Taylor as Ian and I entered our flat in Christchurch with windblown hair. "I see gray," he speculated while reaching for my head.

Brushing his hand away playfully I informed him "Gray hair is a blessing, ask any bald man."

"Where's Madison?" I asked in a worrisome voice, eyeing an unusually empty piano bench.

"He's in the Park with his boyfriend," replied Taylor with a curious flatness.

Turning to Ian I lamented "Our boys are growing up, and soon we'll be all alone."

"Not quite," sang Taylor regaining his mischievous voice. A moment later pandemonium broke out – it was another party at my place.

"Does anyone have the phone number for the Herald, to fend them off?" I pleaded into the crowd.

"Already done, happy birthday dad," crooned Madison, who had appeared hand in hand with his boyfriend, and placed a kiss on my cheek. "They'll be here in a tick," he joked, smiling.

Besides Angles, my flat seemed to have become the other gay venue in Christchurch.

Fortunately for my neighbors, the young and gay are fickle and follow fads. Through attrition, my parties had slimmed to a favorite few couples, no longer worthy of the front page of the Herald.

More specifically, there were five couples who in turn, hosted a dinner at their home once every week. We were a most diverse bunch, and the theme, and food at each particular get together reflected that diversity.

One week it would be pizza and beer in front of the **tellie** in one couple's over crowed, dated lounge.

The next week would be in Spartan surroundings, yet at least at a proper dining table, and the food wholesome New Zealand fare.

When it was my turn to host, it became understood the evening was formal, both in attire and presentation: A throw back to my military days in the wardroom aboard ship?

Perhaps, or perhaps I had been born again as a gay man in New Zealand, and was simply having deja-vu of a previous life.

With most birthdays, one is expected to reflect, or give a speech. I was spared both when Taylor began a raunchy striptease for my guests – and me.

"Once a tart, always..." I muttered which only encouraged him to continue.

When he got down to his speedo, he looked at me, snapped the elastic waistband of the speedo on his smooth skinned thigh, and purred "You want your present now?"

"I'll baptize it *and* you later at the swimming pool," I threatened him, turning away with a wink in Ian's direction.

Turning to face Taylor again, I engaged in fast pursuit of my tart. "But now I'm going to devour you, my sweet," I cautioned him. He did a sloppy pirouette, screamed and began his hasty retreat.

Aidan turned to his flavor of the week, and mouthed wryly to him "The only reason I would take up running, is so I could hear heavy breathing again."

"Childhood is the most precious of all seasons," whispered Ian to himself while eyeing the fun. I had captured Taylor and was administering torture by tickle.

The central city swimming pool in Christchurch was the latest fad venue for gays, although it hadn't been built specifically for us.

Built for the 1974 Commonwealth Games, the pool was at the heart of QEII Park Recreation and Sport Centre, New Zealand's largest multi-sport and leisure complex.

During the next summer months, I would languish in its water. I loved to swim, and proudly displayed Taylor's birthday present.

I would do laps for days in its Olympic sized lanes, and got as tan as a Maori. My hair had grown out, and was bleached blond which ended that brief ethnic association. Exiting the pool I would shake it like a wet dog, and then settle in for a day of sun, fun, and people watching. Chlorine became my aftershave.

Some of the poofters failed to calculate the depth of the water at the diving end, and had to be rescued. I speculated they simply wanted mouth-to-mouth. "No man drowns, who preservers in his prayers, *and* can swim – Russian proverb," I chided one of the survivors, followed by a gentle pat on his back.

"I know, I know," he said recuperating from the ordeal while eyeing my birthday present longingly.

"Seventy five percent of the planet is covered by water, yet you can't swim?" I continued my role as his Jewish mother.

"Do you swim," he began a question in a childlike voice, "because you are too sexy for a sport that requires clothes?"

"Right, cutie, you're going back in the water" I threatened with only a half nudge of my body on his.

There was one person in particular, among all the young cuties, which caught my eye. He always sat half way up the bleachers, near the exit. One day, on the pretext of needing to use the loo, I passed by him at close range and we exchanged nods.

Eventually the nods turned to verbal greetings, and one day I sat next to him.

Now, I loved Ian, and casual sex with this heretofore unknown was not my motive – it was simple curiosity. I sought to further my knowledge of the gay lifestyle.

His name was Bobby. Over time, I had observed that each and every day he left the pool, with a different boy. So, I asked him "How do you do it?"

"Do what?" he replied politely.

"Hook-up with a different guy, every day?" I asked as if a student of Aristotle.

"I don't fear rejection," he replied confidently, "I ask one, if he refuses, then I ask another and another until one says yes," he finished unabashed.

We both looked back at the pool, me nodding appreciatively at the lesson, him looking like a shark searching for its next meal.

Summer lingered, as it should. Laziness found respectability.

As I lay by the pool, I drifted in and out of sleep. The moments awake were filled with the sounds of happy souls around me.

The moments asleep were filled with anguish, as I knew the clock was ticking. My visa was soon to expire.

Suddenly a brisk wind woke me fully, and I was filled with melancholy. "They must constantly change, who would be constant in happiness and wisdom, Confucius," said a voice in my head.

"I'm happy right boldly here," I argued.

"Time is a dressmaker, specializing in alterations," chirped one of the pretties who littered the pool near me. "You talk in your sleep," he finished abruptly before sauntering away.

"Never miss an opportunity to make others happy, even if it means leaving them alone," I jested lightly to his retreating figure. Yet, I was thinking in earnest of my own boys.

Blessed are they
that mourn.

I Told You So

Chapter Thirteen: Down Under

My two boys had flown the nest.

Madison had moved in with the stunner he had been dating monogamously for some time. Their center city flat was tiny, yet they managed to find room for the baby grand piano I gave as a flat warming gift.

At the end of a prolonged farewell hug, I placed Madison's hand into the hand of his boyfriend, as if I were the father of the bride in Westminster Abbey.

My youngest, Taylor had also flown the nest but his relative inexperience flying on his own landed him in a flat directly behind my building.

"At least I can keep a watchful eye," I sighed gratefully, "until he fully matures and can fly further from home."

Angles night club was also in transition. Their lease was about to expire, and a new location for the club had to be sorted out. As a member, I was allowed to participate in the decision making process, but sensed my residual American thinking process was not welcome. "You want to put the new club in the old morgue??" I had dared to blurt out.

Hence, I decided to travel the South Pacific.

I say travel, because a traveler is active; he goes strenuously in search of people, of adventure, of experience. The tourist is passive; he expects interesting things to happen to him. He goes "sight-seeing."

As inexperienced as Taylor was living with a boyfriend, so too was I inexperienced at just being openly gay somewhere other than my birthplace, New Zealand. My first foray would be to relatively close Australia.

My youngest was helping me pack, and advised "When preparing to travel, lay out all your clothes and all your money. Then take half the clothes and twice the money."

"You've moved less than fifty yards from home, and now you're an expert on travel?" I chuckled to myself yet was warmed by his thoughtfulness.

Taylor had tears in his eyes at Christchurch airport, and wouldn't let go of me.

Keeping him purposefully at arm's length, yet still holding both his hands I said firmly, yet softly "Look, son, I'll be back in one month."

"You be safe down under," he spoke now with more composure, and a hint of maturity that stirred my heart.

"You have the keys to my flat," I said reassuringly while patting the pocket of his **long trousers**, "and the key to my heart, always" I finished patting his left cheek, while kissing his right.

Walking the gangway towards the plane, I feared that this had only been a rehearsal for the day I may have to leave New Zealand – forever.

As the plane boarded and we all got settled into our seats, I looked up from having secured my seat belt and noticed four US Servicemen in uniform.

What did I feel? Goodness, a whole bag of emotions that could have torn me apart if I let them.

Instead, I focused on one of the soldiers in particular. He was cute as sin, of course, yet his polite manners set him apart from the other three soldiers. They all had no doubt come up from Antarctica, unless there was a war planned in a nearby island nation that I was no longer going to reconnoiter in advance.

I tried not to stare, but had been transfixed by him when suddenly our eyes met.

He smiled at me, and nodded his head slightly in my direction.

Our gaze was longer than acceptable if we had both been straight men. Then before our connection could become noticeable by his shipmates he was gone.

As he rejoined them, my heart felt for him and what he must be going through inside. I sent him encouraging thoughts.

He too must have studied telepathy at boot camp, because he responded by looking again in my direction, if only for a safe moment.

Having simply flown **across the ditch** I arrived in Sydney, Australia. It would be unlike any place I had seen to date in my world travels. Perhaps because I was now free. I was a new man, and saw everything with a new set of eyes.

"What you've done becomes the judge of what you're going to do - especially in other people's minds. Yet when you're traveling, you are what you are right there and then. People don't have your past to hold against you." ~ William Trogdon, *Blue Highways*.

Mark Twain once said "Travel is fatal to prejudice, bigotry, and narrow-mindedness."

With all due respect, I was not the worry in these regards – it was the people I was about to encounter that scared the crap out of me. "I'm the open minded traveler," I defended myself in advance.

Sure, I had arrived at the point in my life where I could be openly gay, but "there isn't going to be a marching band to greet you everywhere you go," I cautioned myself. "Just because you're free, and gay doesn't mean you will receive a welcome like a returning World War II veteran," I continued to provoke myself.

"If you reject the food, ignore the customs, fear the religion and avoid the people, you might better stay home." ~James Michener.

That's right, James, and I've just landed in Australia, a country of twenty two million people who are entrenched and *who have stayed* at "home."

I needed to narrow my odds of being burned at the stake, and went directly to Oxford Street, Sydney where I could be comfortable among my own, for a start. Perhaps later on this journey I could take Henry Boye's advice; "The most important trip you may take in life is meeting people halfway."

Edward Manor, the name had a quality to it so I checked in. The structure was a reminder of British colonialism, in this now vibrant, modern, alive city.

My room was on the top floor. It had a wood burning fireplace that had already been started, casting a warm glow immediately upon entering. Overstuffed wing-backed chairs and a Chippendale poster bed presided over thick, antique carpets. Worn, yet beautiful wood plank floors struggled for attention. Heavy tapestry window coverings had been drawn open, affording a view of the serene garden at the back of the Manor.

While I could have safely remained in these welcoming surroundings with all their trappings, I yearned to venture "out."

An evening walk down Oxford Street was absolutely overwhelming. Running from Whitlam Square on the south-east corner of Hyde Park in the central business district of Sydney, to Bondi Junction in the Eastern Suburbs, the street is lined with shops, restaurants, and nightclubs.

I would settle in to the western section, which runs through the suburb of Darlinghurst, and is widely-recognized as Sydney's main gay district.

"This all makes Angles in Christchurch, New Zealand look quaint," I mouthed to myself, now standing on a dance floor in an *ocean* of beautiful men. The pulsing beat of the bass sub-woofers went through my body like electric. It competed with the ear popping pounding of my heart in my chest.

"I've never seen this many gay men before," I marveled, eyeing who would be best suited to administer me CPR.

"How many more gay people do the gods have to create before society asks itself whether or not the gods actually want them around?" I rambled while losing all self-control. I was already making wedding plans in my mind with half the men in the room!

Gay marriage was, at this point in society's evolution, still a back burner issue.

Yet, I predicted that the debate would have a religious tone. The people who would testify in favor of banning gay marriage would no doubt be faith leaders using religious arguments.

"If I was Jewish, eating pork or shellfish would not be allowed in my tradition. However, I would never ask the government to impose that religious tradition on my fellow citizens, nor want it subject to popular vote" I rehearsed for this battle that loomed on the horizon.

"You go boy," quipped the voice in my head with a snap of its fingers in the air, "out of the closet for half a tick and already you're taking up arms for gay rights."

"Well, you know me – always in the middle of some conflagration," I snapped right back with unconvincing mock emphasis. I was still a novice with gay mannerisms.

I woke up the next morning, pinching myself for a reality check. "How would my life have differed, if I found all this earlier?" I asked myself.

"You'd probably be dead," said the nemesis in my head. "You were in the military and celibate when the scourge of HIV/AIDS began, hence shielded from its destruction," the voice finished smugly.

Walking down the stairs towards breakfast, I acknowledged the blessing, albeit from a source I had cast off.

I was about to "cast off" more...

Unbeknownst to me, on the ground floor of Edward Manor was one of Sydney's leading gay magazine publishers. Before I had completely dabbed the corners of my mouth with a napkin, from breakfast,

I had been whisked into the publisher's office and found myself nude in front of a camera.

That same night, still reeling from the exposure, I overcompensated and put on several layers of clothing, including a tux and flowing black top coat that made me resemble Darth Vader. I went on a pilgrimage to the famed Sydney Opera House.

It is located in Sydney harbor, and is surrounded on three sides by water. On the fourth side is the Royal Botanical Gardens.

Much more than just an opera house, it has three theatres, a concert hall, a cinema, and exhibition, rehearsal and reception rooms totaling over one thousand.

Its design, of course, contributed to its fame.

Over one million glazed white granite tiles from Sweden covered the roofs, meant to resemble billowing sails on a ship.

So eager was the country for this new national icon, that the government of New South Wales pressed its designer, Jorn Utzon to begin construction – before the design was even complete!

It still took fourteen years to complete, proving you can't rush genius.

Seats for certain performances must be booked well in advance – I hadn't done.

Working my way slowly through the throng towards the box office hoping for the best, I noticed out of the corner of my eye in the distance an important looking entourage emerging from flash cars with valets.

"No time for that," I chided myself, "focus on gaining admission."

Reaching the ticket office with a rapid pulse, I heard "Right, Mr. Bonzo."

I was stunned when the handsome young attendant mysteriously granted me a ticket to a seat in a private box, let alone that he knew my name.

I sensed a few heads turning in my direction moments after I sat in the front row of my box, and as others were seated behind me. I thought "They couldn't have published those pictures in a day!"

The house lights dimmed and all that was forgotten in an instant when I heard a chorus of voices sing "Selig sind, die da Leid tragen." It was the first movement of Ein deutsches Requiem by Brahms – the German Requiem.

At intermission, I could barely move from my seat because I was too embarrassed to be seen with red, teary eyes.

"Blessed are they that mourn," a sole woman's voice from behind me spoke softly in my direction translating into English what we had just heard on stage.

Under normal circumstances I might have turned around in a start, but I was such an emotional wreck that I continued to gaze at the now temporarily empty stage and finished the line in German "denn sie sollen getröstet warden."

Composure regained, I turned slowly and with a start stuttered "Ma'am." I rose from my seat and performed a slight bow.

She extended a familiar white gloved hand and said simply "William."

No doubt it had been her entourage I glimpsed outside earlier, and was of her doing that I got the seat in her box. How she knew I was in Sydney was a mystery to me, yet I shrugged it off and asked her impertinently "Are you still travelling with your two best friends, Louis and Vuitton?"

Her controlled smile born from years of training was none the less as warming to me today as it had been a lifetime ago at Victoria Station.

Bondi Junction Station awaited me now, yet before I left Sydney, I had a love affair – for a day.

We met after the Opera, at a small cafe where he worked, near the Manor where I was staying. I had decided to walk back to my lodging, reflecting on past memories, and new ones and marveled at the overlap.

My Vader look must have appealed to him, and his sheer beauty illuminated the night sky. Waiting for his shift to end, I sat at the café for over an

126   I Told You So

hour. I was completely drinking him in, and he was pleased with my patience.

After we finished our business at the Manor, we settled in each other's arms by the fire in my room.

The following day he was gone. If I were an artist, I could paint his face for you as it is forever embedded in my mind.

I too left Edward Manor that morning for Bondi beach.

Only one kilometer long, it is enclosed north and south by headlands. The beach is ordinary, while the atmosphere is extraordinary; hostels, hotels, shops and restaurants line the promenade full of pavement life. Roller bladders compete for space with dogs that have an attitude. Perhaps this beach walk atmosphere is what endears Bondi with Americans.

Subsequently I went to Manley Beach which is only ten kilometers from Sydney - but a thousand kilometers from care.

It is a more relaxing getaway than Bondi, with small coves and shimmering Norfolk pines. Although, how any gay man could relax here is a mystery to me; sizzling sunshine and a magnificent beach are a magnet for athletic surfer hunks!

I left Manley before I could get into any trouble, and moved on to New Caledonia, were only the Gods know why, I had agreed to holiday for a week with Aidan.

Monsieur, we have information for you.

I Told You So

CHAPTER FOURTEEN: THE FRENCH CONNECTION

A mere 1,500 kilometers (930 miles) east of Australia, New Caledonia was a world apart.

It was a territory of France, even though the very name Caledonia was the Roman word for Scotland! It might well have been called New South France if Captain Cook hadn't "discovered" it in 1774 and given it the Roman name.

The only commonality with Australia was that both countries had been penal colonies.

Indeed, if Napoleon III hadn't finally gazumped the British in 1853 and annexed the island to establish a French penal colony, New Caledonia might have become part of the Commonwealth.

"So," I concluded while tripping down the roll-up stairs next to my propeller driven air craft, "If you broke the law in Britain, or France you got sent to the South Pacific – free."

"If you go afoul of American authority," I continued my self- tutorial, "You arrive at a fog surrounded rock in the San Francisco Bay."

As modern as Sydney had been, Noumea was not.

The café culture was apparent, and appealing; the port picturesque. It was a nice mix between colonial, and island lifestyle.

Not much English is spoken in "Nouvelle-Caledonie" outside the travel industry. The indigenous Melanesians of New Caledonia, the Kanaks, have their own languages but speak French, too. Although the Kanak French accent is slightly pithier than the classic accent in France, the New Caledonian accent generally is neutral.

Its French culture was familiar to me, but not the gay aspect of it. Perhaps that is why I had agreed to holiday here with Aidan, as it was his yearly hunt; I mean haunt.

"How are my boys?" I asked immediately upon greeting him at the airport.

I had arrived a day earlier to reconnoiter.

"Fine, fine" he dismissed the question tersely which indicated he still hadn't gotten into their pants.

"Did you fly here?" he asked stupidly.

"Yea, and boy my arms are tired!" I replied with equal cognitive deficit.

"No, mate" he began his defense unaware of my mockery, "I know you feel about airplanes the way I feel about diets; they are wonderful things for other people to go on."

"Well, you know..." I continued the banter, "The Admiral's yacht was booked so..."

The hotel he routinely stayed at in the hills above Noumea was a dive. Perhaps this is what he had hoped to conceal with the frivolous talk.

"The barracks in Newport looked better than this," I muttered to the roaches fleeing from a giant gecko on the moldy, cracked tiled floor.

"**Quite nice**," I breathed through my teeth to Aidan in full British English while surveying the ruins.

"There's a **torch** here by the door..." he began while proudly showing me the room's attributes.

"Great, let's burn it!" I said in earnest.

"...in case the power fails," he continued unabashed.

"I'll get the **petrol** for the fire," I volunteered unabated, him still unawares.

Our second day, he proudly took me to the "gay" beach to the far, far, far right of Club Med beach.

"If this country used zip codes, this remote portion of the beach would have its own" I said disappointedly to Aidan "Crusoe."

This just wasn't working for me, so I went into town on my own for a café au lait.

Walking a dirt street searching for a café, a Mercedes pulled up and slowed next to me.

"Hello, where are you going?" the driver asked, speaking to my crotch.

"I need to find hospital, to get a cure for this burning sensation when I urinate," I finished my response to his tail lights.

In short order I discovered that Noumea was a banquet of foie gras and frangipani, petanque and palm trees, marinas and mangoes, champagne and geckos, and kisses on both cheeks.

There were boulangeries, patisseries, creperies, boucheries and charcuteries everywhere.

Surrendering at last to the temptation of it all, I chose a café and settled into a relaxing au lait, even though In Noumea, a coffee normally is a short black - and nobody gets takeaway!

In front of the café locals were on cycles with baguettes in their baskets. The supermarket window facing me had full-flavoured cheeses from every French province and was framed with French wine and champagne.

Savouring is one of the things New Caledonians do best, and I embraced it. Day turned to night as I sat there; the balmy evening air was syncopated by music from bars and nightclubs overlooking the lagoon.

Suddenly, the tranquility was punctuated by gun shots.

I poked my head over the railing of the café, hoping to see the Mercedes in flames but was taken aback by uniformed soldiers running in the street.

I reached instinctively for my forty five caliber side arm, but of course, it was no longer part of my body.

I strode out of the cafe with mock calmness, so as not to draw attention to myself, and made it to the British Consulate.

They would make preparations for me to leave the country immediately, but when they saw my name on my passport, fixed their gaze on my face.

"Hey, this fight isn't one of mine," I stuttered at them defensively with a gaze of my own.

My stare was silent reference to all the previous invasions of foreign countries I had participated in.

As further proof that I had come in peace I raised two empty hands in the air. "See, no guns," I half joked.

"Monsieur Bonzo, we have information for you – your father has died," they revealed sympathetically.

"What, in the gun fight outside?" I asked sarcastically, if not nervously, glancing out the window of the consulate towards the now embattled streets of Noumea.

After some time, we managed to make phone contact with my cousin who among other things, asked if I'd be coming home for the funeral.

"Do you hear the gunfire on my end?" I asked her incredulously.

"I have heard gunfire every time you've called me over the years," she replied matter-of-factly.

"True," I had no choice but to agree.

Shouting back into the phone over the increasing street battle noise I said "Tell my sister, after selling the house to just send me a check."

"Where to?" she pressed for the address, neither questioning for a second my not coming home nor inquiring about the raging battle she probably thought I had just started in New Caledonia.

"Christchurch," I supplied, "Cheers."

Handing the phone back to the stunned consulate clerk, I grabbed my passport and made my way to the airport before, I feared, it would be closed by the rebellion.

"War doesn't decide who is right, only who is left," I reflected as I rushed to leave this country.

"All the *arms* I have now, are used for hugging," I rewarded myself as I pressed on furtively for the airport.

"What the world needs is more mistletoe, and less missile-talk," I worked myself into frenzy, with mounting concern that I may be stranded on this powder keg of an island.

"Where to, Monsieur?" asked the ticket agent.

"Whatever is leaving the soonest," I responded, having forgotten Aidan until asked if I had any baggage.

Indecision becomes decision, with time.

Chapter Fifteen: Finding Myself in Fiji

Having survived a civil war in New Caledonia, I would find myself both literally and figuratively in Fiji.

I felt lost.

Nonetheless, it was good to feel lost... because it proved I had a navigational sense of where home was.

"Your compass must be broken then," I informed myself while looking out over the Pacific Ocean, "because it seems to be pointing to Hawaii."

Curious isn't it that I had to leave the comfort of metropolitan Christchurch, only to find my own intuition in the wilderness of Fiji.

My private **bure** was on a remote one of the islands that comprise Fiji. It had a high thatched roof of intricately woven coconut fiber cord sinnet called magi magi used to bind the hardwood poles. Woven matting or bamboo was used as a lining or cladding to the timber construction.

It had no electricity, was surrounded by lush tropical flowers, shrubs and trees, and was just a few feet from the water's edge. A hammock and an outdoor shower completed the idyllic setting. There was something extraordinarily enjoyable about bathing in the open air below a starlit sky or in the daytime with coconut palm fronds dancing in the breeze.

I would spend days, just sitting, and thinking, staring blankly at the water. I reflected that life in general was like the weather here; sometimes sun, sometimes rain. My idleness and unmoving limbs gave the appearance that I was dead, but inside my thoughts were quite alive.

I expected that my migration to New Zealand would be denied. I sensed that very soon I would be forced to leave what had become my re-birth place and what felt like home.

Jean de La Fontaine wrote that a person often meets his destiny on the road he took to avoid it.

"I'm not avoiding a bloody thing," I shouted to a turtle that had crawled to a halt in the sand at my feet. "I'm trying like hell to stay in New Zealand, which is my destiny!" I continued the philosophical discussion with my new friend who was a very good listener.

"Listen to the wisdom of the toothless one, Fijian proverb," I imagined he said. Almost everyone in Fiji speaks English as it is the official language.

Although, unlike Hawaii where English was adopted by gun-point, and the Hawaiian language banned, here it was spoken by choice.

"A friend of yours?" I heard a female voice from behind.

"Why are women always sneaking up behind me?" I begged for a response from my short four legged friend at my feet.

Turning, I was greeted by a smile on the face of the most beautiful female body on the planet. "Are you an angel?" I asked humbly and out loud.

"No," she responded with an even broader smile, revealing perfect teeth. "I too am trying to find myself," she said in a sincere voice.

"You've been eavesdropping," I snapped.

"You've been talking out loud, to a turtle," she jousted.

"Touché," I conceded.

"I know well what I am fleeing from, but not what I am in search of," she spoke mysteriously. She looked out over the water, then back at me with another of her endless, radiant smiles.

It was my turn to look over the water for inspiration, and I added to our conversation "One of the hardest decisions I'm having is to know which bridge to cross, and which one to burn."

"Indecision becomes decision with time," she whispered, laying a hand softly on my shoulder.

We became fast friends, the three of us spending our days by the water, talking, thinking, then talking some more. I honestly can't remember ever sleeping.

The only breaks we took were for swims together, the three of us, and to eat. I knew I had only booked a week at this island, but lost all track of time.

"I could stay here forever," I said leisurely one day.

"Endurance is frequently a form of indecision," she remarked cleverly continuing our conversation from days before as we strolled from the water towards my bure.

I liked the way the breeze ruffled her long, blond hair. It seemed to sway in rhythm with the palm trees. The colorful, light weight, cotton beach wrap she wore around her waist flowed behind her as she walked. It was a *sulu*, the traditional Fijian version of a sarong. Her perfect, yet not rigid posture as she walked furthered the illusion that she was an angel.

Walking side by side, suddenly the beach became our dance floor. I whipped through a triple turn, and then dropped to my knees. Arising to her awaiting hands my partner's skirt spun into a blur as her legs sliced the air. All that was missing was the music of a trovador.

Exhausted from our fun, she took her place beside me in one of two wooden beach chairs in front of my bure, and that faced the ocean. We languished, and surveyed our island kingdom.

The only indication of time was the sun on the horizon.

Sunset was anticipated like an old friend, but no two sunsets were alike.

One evening the sun could peek from behind dense horizon clouds; on another, a cascade of brilliant beams could drown the distant islands in light.

"It's only when we silent the blaring sounds of our daily existence that we can finally hear the whispers of truth that life reveals to us," she remarked as we awaited our friend.

"That blaring sound you heard was my stomach – let's go eat!" I broke the mood. "We'll be back in time for sunset," I assured her, extending my hand in invitation.

Another smile, a whisk of her blond hair out of her eyes, and we were on our way with a skip in our step to retrieve the basket of supplies that were deposited on the island for us daily. They came via a ferry crossing from Vanua Levu, Fiji's second largest island.

On the road Fijian men and women waved their bundles of taro, smiled, and shouted "*Bula!*" (Hello, happy life). We slowed down to exchange greetings with joyful children, inquiring about their rugby scores. It was easily realized that the rhythms of island life brought peace and happiness to the children's faces.

I told one of them that yesterday I had spotted a cow in the rainforest, miles from the village and I asked "How will the cow find its way home?"

"It *is* home," he said.

Reaching the delivery point, we also discovered for once the delivery man sitting in the sand by the basket. He too wore a sulu, and a shirt as Fijians dress modestly at all times.

No hats, no sun glasses, no tank tops as they are considered rude.

"Monsieur Bonzo?" he half asked, half told me.

"Yes, that's me, what's up?" I asked in surprise, while doing an inventory of remaining living relatives in my head, and the food in the basket.

"It is time for you to go home, monsieur," he informed me flatly.

Turning to look my platonic girlfriend in the eyes, I told him from the back of my head "Yes, yes it is."

Was she my muse? Well she wasn't one of the daughters of Zeus, she was quite real, even god-like; an inspiration? Yes, without my even knowing it. Every syllable that left her lips could, in a dull film, make banal voiceover narration sound like velvety wisdom to live by.

On the first day she had walked down the path to my bure all I had seen was her super model beauty.

Now upon our separation, I realized that one of my greatest discoveries on this tiny island had been her inner beauty, which was as radiant as the sunsets we had enjoyed together.

In the end, we were just two pals who enjoyed each other's company, and a moment in time.

I had also discovered that regardless of their situation, Fijians were more than willing to make me feel welcome; it was one of the friendliest and most hospitable places I had ever visited.

Fiji could accurately be called the 'Nation of Smiles and Waves' because they are given abundantly, and freely.

Now, it was mine to smile and wave farewell to them.

There was no
pretending, no hiding.

Chapter Sixteen: An Invitation to the Rose Garden

After Fiji, I returned home to Christchurch. The time I would be allowed to remain in New Zealand was now an ever present distraction. Even so, I would carry on – routine would be my solace, for now.

It was my turn to host the weekly dinner get together. To compensate for my absence, I would change the venue and treat everyone to the rose garden tea house in Hagley Park. Ian couldn't make it up from Dunedin, but comforted me on the phone. He was well able to not only read me, but to read between the lines. "Change is inevitable," he said softly over the wire.

"Except from a vending machine," I quipped in weak protest.

My boys had settled into their own domestic routines in their own homes, to my great delight and relief.

Aidan had managed to get out of New Caledonia without being shot, I learned begrudgingly. His first day back in Christchurch he approached me directly at the gym and spat "You bugger."

"You beguiled me with talk of a holiday, yet you started a war!" he continued his frontal assault.

While he was a despicable old troll of younger men, his hormones did not otherwise make him a mean person at heart. Hence I responded simply, in the native tongue of New Caledonia "Pas moi!" He retreated from his position to a chest press machine, my subterfuge successful.

The invitations to tea would be to the remaining four couples in my dinner circle of friends, and me.

Confucius said "They must often change, who would be constant in happiness or wisdom."

"I don't get it," I said defiantly with one tear rolling down my cheek as I finished addressing the invitations, alone in my flat.

"Continuity gives us roots!" I argued out loud to no one.

"Change gives us branches, letting us stretch and grow," I heard Taylors voice at the doorway to the flat. In an instant I was in his arms, sobbing uncontrollably. "Dad, grow up" he chided from his position a full twelve inches below me.

"Right," I coughed a reply, straightening myself and wiping tears from my face.

The invitations nearly didn't make it, nor did I, as Taylor insisted on going with me to deliver them. He wanted to learn how to drive my Spitfire.

"Slow down," I pleaded.

"Why?" he shouted boldly.

"Because one should never drive faster than one's guardian angel can fly!" I begged.

In New Zealand, one can get a license to drive a car at age fifteen...is considered a man at age sixteen...and only the gods knew, while I feared, what Taylor would be doing after that.

"Son, if you make it to age twenty, the ground will shake," I yelled towards him, the wind in the topless Spitfire taking my words and tossing them in the air as we raced towards...

"A car speeding down the highway loses control, goes through a guard rail, rolls down a cliff, bounces off a tree, lands upside down and finally stops, wheels spinning in the air, smoke and steam pouring out from under the hood," I began a story while clutching the dash of my Spitfire.

"A passing motorist, who witnessed the entire accident, helps the near death, lifeless driver out of the wreck," I continued with increasingly bated breath as Taylor continued to accelerate.

"Got it, dad" Taylor spoke facing me, as my head motioned with raised eye brows towards the road in front of us where his attention ought to be.

Strolling with my youngest through Hagely Park towards the tea house, both with Elvis hair because of the drive, it occurred to me out loud that "if nothing ever changed, there'd be no butterflies."

"The butterfly counts not months but moments, and has time enough," I heard Madison's voice. We embraced with warm pats, while both turning to watch his shirtless boyfriend do back flips in the grass.

His chiseled, dark skinned chest was adorned only by a **hei matau** that swung in unison with his long black hair as his athletic form seemed to defy gravity.

"Teaching Taylor to drive, I see," Madison commented matter of factually while turning his gaze from his boyfriend for just a moment, long enough to eye our hair.

"Not at all," I quip, "I was learning how to swear!" I ignored his gaze, and was accessing his boyfriend's antics.

"Hey dad," Taylor chirps defensively, "I did all right."

"Just remember, son" I began my assessment of his driving skills, "Turn signals are not clues as to your next move in road battle."

We engaged in a mock boxing match, ending with straightening of each other's hair while waiting to be presented to Madison's boyfriend.

"How are you two?" I asked less paternally, yet now more as a friend while we watched the acrobatics.

"Well, I've got all my **chops for a Barbie**, but he seems to be a few **crumbs short of a biscuit**, doesn't he?" Madison quipped.

I smiled to myself because I actually understood what he had said; "I'm all there, but he seems to be neuron impaired," I translated in my head.

"Speaking of food," I responded gentlemanly, "Join us for tea?" "There's a **pavlova** with your name on it!" I appealed to his cravings while licking my lips.

His boyfriend finally had his feet firmly on the ground, and greeted me with a **hongi.**

He strolled hand in hand with Madison through the park and chided me with "**Tu Meke**, but no sweets for him," while rubbing Madison's stomach through the thin, white cotton **singlet.**

"Beware, Madison" I spoke with mock foreboding while observing the rubbing, "that he is not placing a **makutu** on you!"

Taylor's boyfriend had finished work, and joined us in the park. He was a teenaged boy with spiked hair, nose ring, and baggy clothes. Sensing my stare, he offered matter of factually "I don't really like to dress like this, but it keeps my parents from dragging me everywhere with them."

They entered a huddle as we all walked, and were overheard to be discussing how to drive a car.

"Remember," his boyfriend instructed, "the faster you drive through a red light, the smaller the chance you have of getting hit."

Once again sensing my stare, now enhanced with wide eyes, Taylor's boyfriend offered the olive branch by asking me "Do you have women in the American military, sir?"

"Of course we have women in the military, son," I accepted his offer, "and we put them in the front lines."

"Fair dinkum," he responded in amazement, revealing his origins from across the ditch with his accent.

"And they can kill," I continued proudly. "All I have to do is walk over to the women and say; you see the enemy over there? They say you look fat in those uniforms."

As we approached the tea house, I commented that the well-manicured rose gardens resembled more French, than an English garden. "The latter are usually an attempt to blend into the natural landscape, growing a little on the wild side, and preferring not to be molded into perfection," I mused in self-reflection.

"A metaphor of your life?" said Madison.

"Speaking of perfection," Taylor belted out, "Look who's here!" he followed with a head nod through the octagon shaped building with glass on all sides.

In addition to those invited, there was another – Ian.

Seeing my surprise, since I hadn't formally invited him because of his work schedule, he smiled in response to my gaze and said with mustered sarcasm "Well, you never write."

"Ugh?" I began my defense.

"How was your *vacation* in the South Pacific?" he queried politely.

"Ugh, good," I managed two words together, as if we were meeting for the first time all over again.

"That business in New Caledonia," he began evenly, "Were the Americans involved?"

I stifled a laugh, while looking at him and the others awaiting my response.

Straightening my hair yet again, I bought time to come up with "You know, only in America do we have a General in charge of the post office and a Secretary in charge of defense, so who knows what really happened there!"

Dismissing my ruse, Ian embraced my boys with warm hugs and kisses all around.

Notwithstanding his own maneuver at subtly changing a conversation, I chirped "I have been teaching Taylor to drive, hence our hair."

"Really?" he smiled, rustling Taylor's hair even further with his hand.

"Yea, mate," Taylor beamed at Ian enjoying the attention, "and dad saw a sign along the road that said; Dog for sale, eats anything and is fond of children."

"Right, Taylor Saint John," I rebutted, "and any child can tell you that the sole purpose of a middle name is so he can tell when he's really in trouble."

My left hand met Ian's in Taylor's hair, while my right hand embraced Ian's waist and pulled him close.

We were seated inside the leaded glass dome that was the tea house, when our pots of tea arrived almost immediately. The food came sometime thereafter on three tiered trays; top tier was scones, middle tier was savories and finger sandwiches, and the bottom tier was sweets.

Taylor reached for a scone, and began cutting it horizontally with a knife. I coughed in his direction, got his attention, and then prepared my own. The correct manner in which one eats a scone is the same manner in which one eats a dinner roll. Simply break off a bite-size piece, place it on your plate, and then apply, with your bread and butter knife, the jam and cream. A fork is not used to eat a scone. Please, no dipping!

"Right, ta dad," he said with a smile and upturned nod.

"And the tea?" asked Madison having seen the lesson for properly eating a scone, "is it milk before, or after the tea has been poured?"

"Ah ha," I over emphasized theatrically, "What to do with the milk?"

"Yee gods," groaned Ian with a playful roll of his eyes.

"Originally all tea cups in Europe were made from soft paste porcelain," I began my thesis, "The milk was added first to temper the cups from cracking."

"Once hard paste porcelain was discovered in Europe by Bottger in 1710, for the Meissen Porcelain factory, it was no longer necessary to temper the cups. Hence, it made more sense to add milk after the tea has brewed," I continued to my wide eyed pupils.

"Why?" came from Madison's boyfriend beneath his raised hand.

"As we are all aware," I happily replied, "in Her Majesty's Empire the correct brewing of tea is judged by its color, therefore milk after is a wiser choice."

"So, mate" began Taylor's boyfriend with half a laugh ending the tutorial, and taking the conversation in a different direction, "how was your trip across the ditch?"

"Yes, pray tell?" Ian spoke while surveying every face at the table, then me making the question ubiquitous.

"Our plane was taking off from Christchurch Airport," I began at the beginning to great guffaws and groans from my listeners. Even the waiter seemed concerned with the length the story might be, shooting me a quick look.

"After it reached a comfortable cruising altitude," I persisted unabated, "The pilot made an announcement over the intercom: 'Ladies and gentlemen, this is your captain speaking. Welcome to Flight Number 293, nonstop from Christchurch to Sydney. The weather ahead is good and we should have a smooth and uneventful flight. Now, sit back and relax - OH MY GOD!'"

"Dead silence followed on the intercom," I stopped to ascertain the equally silent, yet none the less attentive audience in the tea house.

"After a few minutes," I continued, "the pilot came back on the intercom and said, 'Ladies and Gentlemen, I am so sorry if I scared you earlier. But, while I was speaking, the flight attendant brought me a cup of hot coffee and spilled the coffee all over my lap. You should see the front of my pants!'"

"I shouted back towards the cockpit; that's nothing, you should see the back of mine!" I finished my story to a round of applause punctuated with laughter.

Sitting down next to Ian, I earned a kiss, either for the humor of my story, or its brevity.

Everyone neared the bottom of their cups, the trays had been emptied and the waiter busied himself. I watched it all contentedly, if not from a third person perspective.

While I had partaken of Tea in many elegant places around the world, I had usually been alone. This time it was different, I was with family. It had also been a relatively simple affair, simplicity being the ultimate sophistication.

The tables had been cleared. The guests were now void of all obligations, save that of their own leisure.

Madison and his boyfriend lingered nearby. They were either practicing some sort of mixed martial arts, or having their first argument. I began to rise from my chair to assist, when Ian placed a gentle, restraining hand on my arm.

Taylor and his boyfriend went in another direction. They were examining each other's body, in what looked like a plan for additional piercings. I began to rise from my chair to assist, and felt Ian's hand holding me back once again.

"Is there a spring loose in your chair?" he asked, releasing his grip on me.

"You're right," I responded only to his hand gestures, "It's time to let go."

I had built a family in New Zealand, person by person. It had taught me that a family need not be defined by those with whom we share blood, but by those for who we would give our blood.

My happiness was a gift. I hadn't expected it, but now delighted in it.

I Told You So

CHAPTER SEVENTEEN:
THE WIZARD FORESEES

"Take one step forward

And I shall stay still,

Vast spaces far apart

I don't have to see you,

To know our love is real."

"Write me a letter

For my eyes to read,

Emotions and feelings utter

My mind shows me,

What my heart needs is you."

"One day we'll be together

Face to face standing before each other,

Smiling touching feeling closer

One kiss to heal longing torture,

One look to see love and know its forever."

"**Werlu Angeles**," The Wizard finished from his perch on his wooden ladder, in the center of Cathedral Square. He looked spent and leaned on the handrail for a moment's breathe before continuing in another vein.

"My God: was that about us?" I turned and quizzed Ian who had been, as always, at my side when I needed him.

"It's not unimaginable," said Ian without interrupting his gaze towards The Wizard, "in 1963 he graduated from the University of Leeds with a double honors degree in psychology and sociology."

Looking back towards the wizard in awe, I got his attention with a simple lift of my eyebrows, and spoke with a philosophical voice "A man with one watch knows what time it is; a man with two watches is never quite sure."

"Even a clock that does not work is right twice a day," he responded half to me, and the other half to the rest of audience." Their applause declared him the victor of our joust, which I acknowledged with a respectable bow in his direction.

"Have the plans for the party been finalized? All the invites sent?" Ian asked softly as he led me gently to a bench in the square.

Glancing at the Wizard, who I still see but not hear from our distance, I said "Ask the Wizard, he seems to know all; I'm **two sammies short of a pic nic**."

With a gentle nudge in my side, Ian prodded me towards Drexel's which was to be the venue for one last hooray! "Let's talk to Norm and Julie, and make sure it's all sorted," he said wisely.

"They've sold the restaurant, you know," I informed Ian.

"Yea, all these years I thought they were mysterious and turns out they're just plain crackers," I continued with a laugh. "But," I moaned while rubbing my stomach, "I enjoyed the investigation!"

Ian's wrinkled brow indicated more explanation was needed.

"The two of them are going around the world – on a tandem bike!" I offered further explanation.

"And what of that *mysterious man* they were always forcing you to share a table with at breakfast, after your gym work-out?" he puzzled.

"Ah, the *mystery man*," I began my labored response. However, the restaurant was looming before us now and I was spared a detailed response.

I abbreviated; "He works for the US Government."

"That's all?" pleaded Ian, "Now you're being mysterious," he chuckled while holding the door open for me.

"Oooooooooo," I feigned a secretive voice, while my fingers did a dance from his waist up to his nose, which I pinched then said "Let's eat."

"Hey, Norm," we greeted the owner with bated breath, not from walking but in anticipation of another great meal at Drexel's.

"William, Ian," he responded with brevity, yet accompanied by a warm smile. His haste was born only from the fact that the restaurant was, as usual, packed with hungry patrons.

Notwithstanding, he paused to afford us a moment when I asked, "If your dog is barking at the back door and your wife is yelling at the front door, which do you let in first?"

"The dog of course," he quickly replied without hesitation or thought, "at least he'll shut up after you let him in."

Norm continuing his rounds, Ian and I sat. "The restaurant may remain, but there will always only be one Norm and Julie Drexel" I sighed as Ian and I barely glanced at the familiar menus.

While enjoying, this my last breakfast at Drexel's, I had time to formulate a response to Ian's earlier inquiry regarding with whom I had shared my table on so many previous occasions.

"You see how packed this place always is?" I began between mouthfuls.

His survey of the buzzing restaurant was followed with nods, and a fresh mouthful of his own.

"Well, I would always show up, party of one..." I continued, "...then mystery man would always show up, alone..." I prepared for the punch line, "and Bob's your Uncle, we were seated together..."

"...to save tables," Ian provided unconvinced.

"Yes!" I exclaimed.

For emphasis I added "Yet there weren't always tables enough even for us, so frequently we would volunteer to eat on the stoop outside the back kitchen door..."

"...next to the dust bins?" Ian finished another one of my sentences flatly with a doubtful tilt of his head.

"Yep," I concluded in a deflated voice indicating imminent surrender.

"When foreign, sovereign nations say there are Americans everywhere, they hope it to be hyperbole," he provided his well worded summation.

We turned from that discussion, back towards our food. From the corner of my eye, I glimpsed a drunken man get up from his table and stumble towards the bathroom. "No doubt he spent the night clubbing and hasn't even been home yet," I whispered to Ian.

A few minutes later, a loud, blood-curdling scream was heard coming from the bathroom.

A few minutes after that, another loud scream reverberated through the restaurant, stealing everyone's attention in that direction.

Norm hastily went towards the bathroom to investigate what the drunk was screaming about.

"What's all the screaming about in there? You're scaring my customers!" he asked with concern in his voice with an ear to the door.

"I'm just sitting here on the toilet and every time I try to flush, something comes up and squeezes the hell out of my balls," the man exclaimed from within.

With that, Norm opened the door, looked in and said, "You idiot! You're sitting on the mop bucket!!!"

Some moments later, the man emerged from the bathroom, and stumbled towards the exit of the restaurant with fixed determination. Yet, as he passed Ian and me, he paused with a start, turned towards us directly, placed both his hands on our table in order to brace himself, and shared secretly with us in half a whisper, "Did you hear about the red ship and the blue ship that collided?"

"Yes," I whispered into his ear, "the survivors were marooned."

After he had bolted through the front door, it was now forever off kilter. Ian sat upright and asked me squarely, "Your American contact?"

"Norm?" I motioned silently towards the kitchen with an upheld cup indicating more coffee, please.

Ian continued the mime routine I had started by tapping his right index finger onto his left wrist, indicating that we needed to get a move on as the movers would be arriving at my flat soon.

"Norm?" I wrote in the air with an invisible pen, now needing the check instead.

I broke the silence with, "Why do people point to their wrist when asking for the time, but don't point to their crotch when they ask where the bathroom is?"

It will be a costume party, period.

I Told You So

Chapter Eighteen: Absolutely Fabulous Farewell

My furniture had been picked up by the military for shipment out of New Zealand. My flat in Christchurch was empty. There was nothing on the walls save empty picture hooks, nothing on the floors but scraps of packing tape. The front lounge resembled a crime scene, the missing nine foot long Broadwood piano leaving a dustless impression on the wood floor. The two-way swinging doors between the kitchen and dining room were propped open for easy removal of boxes with their contents. My boys would not be running through them anymore.

The silence was deafening.

It was a stark contrast to my life the last three years in New Zealand which had been lived to the fullest for the first time!

In reflection, one often employs offensive cultural caricatures – I could not, as there were none in or about New Zealand, save perhaps me!

At good old 76 Lichfield Street, in the quiet mid-afternoon hours sun poured through the windows at the top of the stairs, sashes open fully and curtains drawn aside. No attempt was being made to hide the damp, dank, dark interior that was otherwise Angles nightclub. The dance floor was void of life. Yet, a cacophony was taking place in the front lounge.

After too much debate it was decided "It will be a costume party, period" I ended abruptly the colorful discussion. Once animated faces now stared at me with a frozen gaze and speechless, gaping mouths.

After I had left the party planning meeting on foot, having sold my Harley, the discussion reanimated excitedly and my decision was translated and morphed into a "Period costume party!"

The print media had been notified that the Yank was at it again. The dialogue penned for the characters wouldn't be without heart or interest, but would seem much ado about little until spoken by the likes of the Herald! This final event of my life in New Zealand would come to be billed as an "Absolutely Fabulous Farewell."

On the appointed day, Police took up position at both ends of Hereford Street. Suddenly the horse-drawn carriages began to appear. Their clop, clop, clopping sound slowed to a stop in front of Drexel's restaurant. It was replaced by clapping of bystanders and gawkers.

When the guests began to descend from their respective carriages, I leaned sideways towards Ian, covered my mouth with my hand and said "What *Period* are they going for?"

"Shush," he hissed pinching me, continuing without interruption to take in the spectacle, "This has all been acted out for you."

A single frame picture would struggle to capture persons adorned with twelve to twenty four inch tall masses of white hair. Faces were powdered white and completed with paste-on beauty marks. Rivers and rivers of fabric flooded Hereford Street. All were greeted by white gloved valets in resplendent uniforms.

I smiled politely towards everyone, while calculating incredulously if there was a single sequin left for purchase in the free world.

"I don't think even the Herald was prepared for this," I muttered once again towards Ian.

"Oh look," Ian shook my arm with his left hand, while pointing excitedly to one of the carriages just arriving with his right hand. It was Taylor and his boyfriend, and Taylor was wearing a military uniform, *and* my Navy sword.

"If he ever enlists for real, he'll be a real heart breaker," I predicted.

Inside Drexels the party had begun, as the carriages outside continued to arrive and depart.

Entering the mayhem, one guest who had started to party *early* stumbled towards Ian and I and managed to blurt directly at me "The Queen and The Pope got nothing over you, mate."

I paused for a tick, to consider if he meant that their previous visits to New Zealand had been less spectacular than mine, or if they had no evidence of anything I may be summoned to explain!

Suddenly, violins could be heard throughout the restaurant, and I thought out loud "Ah, Vivaldi."

"Actually, it's Aqua," chirped Taylor, who had appeared suddenly, poking me from behind with my own sword, and playfully grabbing my hands and leading me to into the throng that had begun to move to the sound of *Barbie Girl*.

My recollections of the day's events get blurry from there on...

One Christchurch policeman had waited outside the restaurant, if not for our safety, then hoping for a bust.

At closing time everyone came out and he spotted his potential quarry. The young man was so obviously inebriated that he could barely walk. He stumbled around the parking lot for a few minutes, looking for his car.

Although most had arrived by carriage, many had driven from the environs.

After trying his keys on five other cars, he finally found his own vehicle. He sat in the car a good ten minutes.

He turned his lights on, then off, wipers on, then off. He started to pull forward onto the sidewalk, and then stopped. Finally he pulled out into Hereford Street and started to drive away.

The policeman, waiting for this, turned on his lights and pulled the young man over a block away on Park Terrace. He administered the breathalyzer test, and to his great surprise, the man blew a 0.00.

The policeman was dumbfounded. "This equipment must be broken!" he exclaimed.

"No, it isn't," giggled Taylor from the window of my Spitfire, "I'm the designated decoy!"

THE END

Everyone has gone. Party favors litter the floor, unwashed glasses line the bar. Yet, I'm thankful for the mess because it means I had been surrounded by friends.

An odd silence is punctuated only by the occasional delivery **lorry** passing in Hereford Street in the now quiet, early morning hours. I also hear Ian's breathing as he puts his arms around me from behind.

Taking one of his hands in mine, I lead him towards a small upright piano in the corner of the restaurant, removing further evidence of the evening's frivolity with a flick of my free hand. I guide him gently down to the bench, and then begin to play pianissimo, with a sense of reflection.

"Crazy world," I sing softly, "full of crazy contradictions like a child," I continue looking only at the keys. From the closeness we have shared, he knows instinctively this is not about him – but about what was the greater part of my life, the military.

"Just when I believe your heart's getting warmer, you're cold and you're cruel, and I, like a fool, try to cope, try to hang on to hope; crazy world,"

I finish, turning towards him and looking into his eyes.

He leans his head onto my chest, acknowledging silently that my life in the military, and in New Zealand were at an end. We are full of each other, but I am empty inside aware that my attempt to immigrate to New Zealand after leaving active duty had failed.

I went to the airport alone, not wanting to be seen a sobbing mess.

Finding my seat on the plane, I sat with a thud. I was numb yet tingling all over.

I hadn't fully appreciated the depth of my love for this country, these people until this our moment of separation.

The pilot and co-pilot seem to be against me as well as the United States military and immigration laws, as they push the throttle forward and slam me against the back of my seat. The roar of the engines thankfully masks the sound of my sobbing.

In short order, at five hundred miles per hour, the distance between me and New Zealand, me and Ian, me and my boys, me and my first gay friends grows incalculable.

Trying to comfort myself, I slip on my headphones and play The Four Seasons by Vivaldi. It's soothing, yet at the same time leaves me longing. It can't bring back all that I have left behind.

Closing my eyes does little to change the emptiness and darkness that surrounds me, but separates me from it if only by the thin layer of skin that is my eyelids.

In this vague retreat, I equate my military life with winter because I was unable to grow as a person.

What was "The bountiful harvest of autumn?" you ask. That is all the people I was enriched by, in the land of the Kiwi.

I would never see any of them again; in part because of my personal conviction to not look back in life, and in part because tragically, many of them would not survive the earth quake of February, 2011 that would shake Christchurch to its very core.

My memories of New Zealand never fail to put a smile on my face, and they will be how I remember New Zealand, until I die.

Suddenly, the sun bursts through the plane window and forces me to open my eyes. We have been travelling east, and yesterday has become today again. The seasons are going in reverse.

I am going home – home to Hawaii, where it is perpetually summer.

EPILOGUE

Raising myself from the lawn at Punchbowl Crater in Honolulu, Hawaii, my elbows have formed a lasting impression in the grass near Sam.

It hadn't been a story of heroic feats, just a tale of lives that ran parallel for a while. For the first time in my life I had been among persons with whom I had common aspirations, and similar dreams.

I shake my arms to get circulation again while looking towards him and say "Eh brah, know what? I got one more, **dakine**, story to tell."

"For reals?" I imagined hearing him say, "I gonna be da star?"

"Yea, brah!"

I look up and see that the palm tree fauns above Sam and I have begun dancing in the gentle trade winds, inviting me to dance with them and tell the next story.

Before westerners first arrived in the islands, there had been no written language in Hawaii so stories were passed down through the hula. Hula literally means, dance.

Turning back towards Sam, I chide him saying "I can't tell em through dakine, hula, need you for da **kuma**!"

I place a kiss on the palm of my hand, and then place my hand on the ground above him.

"Aloha nui loa, Sam," I whisper for his ears only, "a hui ho."

GLOSSARY

"Easy reading is damn hard writing." ~Nathaniel Hawthorne.

When I was told I should include a glossary by the first critical set of eyes to read *I Told You So*, I was taken aback. "If Shakespeare had had to include a glossary, he'd still be writing *The Two Gentlemen of Verona*!" I snapped at the indignant suggestion.

None the less I set about dutifully and in doing so was myself amazed at the number of words and phrases that readers might not understand. Indeed, if used incorrectly the words and expressions defined herein could result in a faux-pas of international proportions.

For example, my brother's name is Randy. Should he be in Australia or New Zealand and introduce himself by saying "Hello, I'm **Randy**" the results might be quite unintended…

Therefore, for your ease of reading I am pleased to provide you the following words and expressions with their accompanying definitions.

a

across the ditch across the Tasman Sea.

alright a common greeting used in Britain, British Commonwealths, or former British Colonies; usually used in conjunction with the word mate.

Aotearoa most widely known and accepted Maori name for New Zealand, translated as "Land of the Long White Cloud."

Aussie-ockers the term "ocker" is used both as a noun and adjective for an Australian who speaks and acts in an uncultured manner, using a broad Australian accent (or Strine).

b

banger sausage.

bloody cheek damned impudence.

bloke usually a man and often used when referring to a stranger, or used when referring to someone you like.

Bob's your Uncle roughly translates to 'there ya go.'

bog queen toilet; gay man. A gay man looking to have sex in a public toilet.

bonnet car hood.

boondocker US slang for military footwear.

boondocks New Zealand slang for rural area.

boot car trunk.

box of budgies cheerful, happy, very good.

brollie common British Empire word for a proper British umbrella.

bugger off piss off, shove off, get out.

bure Fijian word for a wood-and-straw hut, similar to a cabin.

C

Canterbury a province on the east coast of the South Island of New Zealand.

cheers goodbye or thanks or good luck.

cheerio good bye.

chips french fries.

chops for a Barbie wits about oneself; intact intellect.

corker very good.

crikey! gosh! wow!

crisps potato chips.

crumbs short of a biscuit not all there intellectually.

cuppa cup of tea.

d

dakine can mean anything, either when the exact word you are looking for escapes you, or when you are talking to someone and actual words are not needed as it is understood, from the context of your discussion, what you mean to say. For example, if you and your friend both surf every morning at the crack of dawn, you both show up at da beach at the crack of dawn plus thirty minutes ('cause we all on Hawaii time in the islands) seeing nice waves and say to each other "eh brah, good day for dakine, yea?" It is understood that in this context dakine means surfing!

dinky di Australian Bush Vernacular: To stress truth, speaking for real.

dust-bin rubbish, trash container.

e

eh pronounced as you would the letter "a" and often used at the end of sentences when expecting a response to a statement.

f

fair dinkum Australian slang for fair or true; to proclaim a fact or truth in a statement or as a question; equivalent to American "No shit!"

fizzy soda pop.

flash sensational or "thats flash" meaning it looks really good.

flat apartment.

floozy an offensive term that deliberately insults; vulgar and promiscuous.

g

G & T gin and tonic.

gaydar a sense that allows for someone to detect homosexuality in another; short for gay-radar; the ability to tell when someone near you is homosexual, even if they have given no obvious indications of being so.

give your ferret a run have sex.

good on ya, mate congratulations, well done; expression of approval, friendly approval of somebody's actions.

good as gold a good job; well done; not a problem; an affirmative answer .

guts for garters in big trouble, as in "I'll have your guts for garters!."

h

haere ra goodbye; from Māori, literally: go away!

Haka dance, commonly a war dance.

hard case joker, comedian.

hei matau traditional Maori pendant, made from bone or greenstone carving in the shape of a highly stylized fish hook.

hongi traditional Maori greeting, done by pressing one's nose to another person's nose.

hooray the **Kiwi** "Goodbye."

k

kia ora hello (Maori origin).

Kiwi New Zealander.

kiwi an endangered flightless bird native to New Zealand.

kuma literally means teacher in Hawaiian.

l

Laie a largely Mormon community on the North Shore of Oahu, Hawaii home to the Brigham Young University and right next door to the Polynesian Cultural Center.

L&P fizzy soda water, Lemon & Paeroa (L&P); originally lemon flavoured spring water from the town of Paeroa.

lift elevator.

long-drop outhouse, outdoor loo, shithouse.

long trousers a euphemism for when British school boys transition from wearing short pants and knee socks, to a man's long trousers.

loo bathroom.

loar to praise, or laud.

lorry truck.

m

makuahine Hawaiian for "mother."

makutu bewitch; spell; incantation.

manuhiri a visitor to a **Maori marae**.

Maori indigenous people of New Zealand.

marae flat area of ground in front of a meeting house, place of weighty discussion and consultation.

moko tattooing (on the face or body).

mate buddie (common term, and can be used even with strangers).

n

naff off get lost!

North Carolina Charles L. Worley of Providence Road Baptist Church in Maiden, N.C., condemns President Obama while calling for gays and lesbians to be put in an electrified pen and ultimately killed off.

"Build a great, big, large fence – 150 or 100 mile long – put all the lesbians in there," Worley suggests in a clip, reportedly filmed on May 13 2012.

He continues: "Do the same thing for the queers and the homosexuals and have that fence electrified so they can't get out...and you know what, in a few years, they'll die out...do you know why? They can't reproduce!"

p

pakeha non-Maori person.

pavlova meringue tort, covered in cream and fruit, named after the Russian ballerina Anna Pavlova.

petrol gasoline.

pidgin a simplified language that develops as a means of communication between two or more groups that do not have a language in common. Hawaiian pidgin is a result of Asian plantation workers brought to Hawaii. Later, English speaking Missionaries would infuse (more like impose!) their language into the language mix.

podocarp native New Zealand coniferous hard woods that boast a lineage stretching back to the time when New Zealand was part of the super continent of Gondwana.

poofter Australian/New Zealand slang for a homosexual; a male homosexual, often one who is also effeminate in his mannerisms.

powhiri formal welcome.

q

quite nice a term used when you can't really think of anything better to say; as in "her hat is quite nice," and you often mean the opposite!

r

randy horny, feeling sexy.

rubbish trash or garbage, as in "should I throw this in the rubbish?"

s

sheila Australian slang for "woman" or "female."

she'll be right not a problem, it'll be O.K.

singlet sleeveless under shirt.

sparrow fart very early in the morning - the crack of dawn.

spinner usually used to describe a female who is a little flakey/stupid or even of ill repute.

strewth honestly, expletive showing frustration.

sweet-as a term people say instead of "cool" or "awesome."

†

ta thanks.

taiaha a traditional weapon of the **Maori** of **Aotearoa**. This hardwood weapon is used for close-quarters combat. Though sometimes referred to as a spear-like weapon, the taiaha is not used as a spear. Held with two hands, short, calculated strikes, blocks and thrusts are conducted to intimidate and exhibit the prowess, strength, power and the skill of the Maori warriors.

take-aways New Zealand term for "take-outs" or food "to go."

tangata whenua people of the land, Maori.

tellie television.

tomato sauce catsup.

too right absolutely, certainly; an expression of emphatic agreement.

torch flashlight.

Treaty of Waitangi The English and Māori versions of the Treaty differed significantly, so there is no consensus as to exactly what was agreed to. From the British point of view, the Treaty gave Britain sovereignty over New Zealand, and gave the Governor the right to govern the country. Māori believed they ceded to the Crown a right of governance in return for protection, without giving up their authority to manage their own affairs.

Tu Meke a phrase commonly used by the native people of New Zealand, Maoris, to show that they are impressed or show respect for your actions.

two sammies short of a picnic used to describe a person who is a "bit thick."

U

up the boohai shooting pukeko's with a long-handled shovel lost; lost in the head; slang for far from civilization. The Puhoi is a river just north of Auckland. Over the years the phrase has evolved and is now often heard as "Up the Boohai…"

V

vegemite spread for toast or bread the color of dark molasses, the consistency of cold honey and the flavor of yeasty soy sauce.

W

Waitaki a valley that straddles the boundary between the North Otago and Canterbury provinces.

waka hourua canoe, double hulled. Two single-hull waka taua lashed together.

wellies gumboots.

Werlu Angeles wrote his first poem in the second grade titled "She's a Fucking Bitch to Me" when the most popular girl in the class broke his heart. He graduated high school in Reno, Nevada then subsequently went to college for two years in the Philippines. His forte is love poems, whether the emotion is hate or happiness. However, his most recent (yet untitled) poem was the result of another emotional upheaval of a much different sort - the death of his mother in November, 2011. It is a testament to a strong woman, from a grieving son.

wero challenge by throwing a spear.

wop-wops out of the way location.

Y

yank an American.

you right mate instead of saying how may I help you New Zealander or Australian says "you right mate?"

Z

Zippy's Restaurant a combination fast-food chain and casual dining restaurant in Hawaii which opened in 1966. All locations are on Oahu, with one on Maui for da tourists!

AFTERWARD

The drugstore, like the men's clothing shop next door and the piano shop beyond it are still stocked with products. The now dusty shelves are filled with medications that will never soothe a headache or battle a cold. Clothes will never be worn, and pianos sit like stunned, silent giants. All were abandoned without notice. Christchurch is now the world's largest ghost town. It is a city under siege, its inner heart crumbling.

The destruction is overwhelming. The central business district is still cordoned off. The Christchurch Cathedral, now the symbol of the quake's destructive power is visible to only a select few allowed into the city. More than nine hundred buildings are tagged for demolition. The stadium, the outlet for rugby pride, and where I had once seen the Queen will also probably have to come down.

One of the few habitable hotels is the George on Park Terrace. Just one block away the building where I lived and the flat which was home is gone. Every third or so house seems uninhabited, many bearing the red sticker that signals their likely doom, while many others are simply gone, front steps and letterboxes leading up to vacant lots and piles of rubble.

Aftershocks abound, during which more buildings collapse hindering the recovery.

Cycling and Christchurch have always gone together: it is a flat city with stunning gardens and riverside paths. Pre-quake, it felt like Cambridge, with bikers riding parallel to punts cruising on the Cam-like Avon. Now the damaged roads and cordons give a bike the edge in efficiency, as long as you are prepared for undulating paths.

It is a bucolic, if melancholy ride along the riverside.

The Avon River on whose banks my parties had caused tour busses to halt in their tracks is now an open sewer. The sandy alluvial soil of Christchurch has been liquefied by the quake into a morass of bubbling, glutinous stinking slime. Broken pipes and effluvium from the chemical toilets that remaining residents must use ad to the horrid contents.

It is difficult to feel anything but powerless, because the attacker responsible for all this destruction is Mother Nature.

There is an odd Sunday afternoon feel about this weekday mid-morning as many residents have fled, to stay with relatives or friends elsewhere. Schools all over the country report a boost to enrolments. Others, with equity tied up in damaged houses, await insurance settlements. Some vow they will head for Australia at the first opportunity. Their drive through the western suburbs to the airport will be bumpy on the damaged road jolted out of its usual position when the earth pushed up.

Still, there is life about. Joggers, builders and residents hail one another. Community spirit, I'm told, has grown, as it does in adversity.

In this "the most English of cities outside of Great Britain" the big picture is greater than the destruction. New Zealand's second largest city is undergoing its next evolution as it rethinks, reinvents and rebuilds!

An evening spent in the company of a group of impassioned locals, journalists, writers, musicians, designers, civil servants, and engineers underlines the depth of ideas for the future of Christchurch. Arguably, no-one wants any Auckland-style carbuncles. Instead the talk is of decentralization, low-rise, green buildings, light rail, sustainability.

"Will Christchurch retain its English heritage?" I ask myself.

"No doubt," I answer my own question with a knowing nod, "But it will be a much more modern city." There's real visionary thinking here, real possibilities to do something amazing.

To be sure, the destruction was not confined to Christchurch.

In Lyttleton, the charming and cultured port town across the hills from the city was the epicenter of February's 7.1 quake. A fuel tanker sits abandoned and blocked by fallen rubble on the main road between Lyttelton and Christchurch. Half of the town's handsome colonial stone structures are gone. Above the town, the old timeball station, which used to signal the arrival of ships in port and the time to mariners, is a ruin. Its tower still stands: talk is that it will be restored and partially preserved to mark the disaster.

In Auckland on the north island the damage is to the national psyche. In this the country's largest city, where usually only stories of rugby, hobbits or a whale stranding trouble even the inner sections of the papers published abroad, the airwaves have continued to be abuzz with news of aftershocks in the country's second largest city, Christchurch. The largest which topped 6.3 magnitude during which one hundred and eighty one people died. The images of the destruction to both property and life incapacitate me; I can't move, I can't breathe, as surely as if I had been there.

Yet, I take with me other images as well. One in particular of a white wooden barrier built at the edge of the red zone in Christchurch. It has not been tagged with graffiti. It has simply a picture of Her Majesty's crown and underneath the words "Keep calm, and carry on."

Another image is of the redevelopment of Rugby League Park in Christchurch's inner-west which has allowed The All Blacks rugby tests – the first time they have played in the city since they beat Australia there in 2010.

When the world says "Give up," hope whispers "Try one more time."

You can get *there*, from *here* New Zealand. I know you will...

E noho ra,

William Bonzo